Jokumaraswami

and Other Plays

NEW INDIAN PLAYWRIGHTS

CHANDRASEKHAR KAMBAR

Jokumaraswami

and Other Plays

LONDON NEW YORK CALCUTTA

Seagull Books, 2025

ISBN 978 1 8030 9 524 0

British Library Cataloguing-in-Publication Data
A catalogue record for this book is available from the British Library

Typeset by Manasij Dutta, Seagull Books, Calcutta, India
Printed and bound by WordsWorth India, New Delhi, India

CONTENTS

JOKUMARASWAMI

A Play in Nine Scenes

Translated from the Kannada by
Rajiv Taranath

TRANSLATOR'S INTRODUCTION

An apparently wild opulence is what greets the reader as he delves into Kambar's writings. It is better that the reader relaxes into that opulence. For if he insists on taking a framework of logic into his reading, then that very frame might trip him up.

In play after play, the pivot is a fantasy or a superstition which has the elements of a problem; the play is the working out of the problem in, one notes, importantly, man–woman terms and not husband–wife terms. Indeed, this could be described as a Kambar paradigm in which there is a shift from socially acceptable relationships to more powerful primordial bonds. It recurs in variation in *Jokumaraswami* as well as in *Siri Sampige, Kadu Kudure* and *Rishyashringa,* and is suggested in his poetry as well. The consequences are invariably painful. The tone also always celebrates primordial rather than local and social 'mores'. Nowhere in Kambar do we find extramarital love viewed pejoratively. The Gowdathi–Basanna pairing is the culmination of a logic very different from the routine logic of social propriety. Thus these consummations come through as experiences where the epiphanic joy of the couple coincides with the menace of social propriety, hovering without in the form of ritual torture and death. In this shift from the social to the primitive, Kambar is placing instances side by side and allowing endorsements and rejections to arise naturally.

It is obvious that Kambar's writing teems with images and symbols, and so, one could be tempted into discussing Kambar only in terms of symbolism. In fact, there is something at once more simple, fresh and profound operating. Kambar builds with words which are pieces, stories or pictures, heard or felt dreams, all of which arise from his environment. Indeed, the manner in which he relates to his environment—both in time and in space—is through the stories, fantasies and images that he uses. It is not as if he is trying to relate in a poetic manner something which already exists: outside there is only anonymous stock, plural and characterless like bricks and mortar. In order to internalize it, Kambar must build with it. And in this task, he gives character to his environment and imbibes it again as a writer. They make each other.

He looks around and looks to himself. What he seems to find is always in terms of plentitude—mad joy, shimmering cruelty, pain, sex, loneliness, unbelievable quests by legend-like people in legend-like structures—all of which he celebrates. Celebration is, for Kambar, a primary mode of experience. And because the celebration has a musicality at once private and shared, the rhythm is at once private and contemporary, a blend of the self and the community. In celebrating, Kambar functions crucially as a myth-maker. To recognize him as a myth-maker is to make a crucial identification of the most significant configuration of Indian poetic genius. The Sanatana mythogony is only a very small part of the dark and passionate world in which Kambar makes his space. Myth celebrates, philosophy contemplates. The mythical episteme is one of recognition as growth. The philosophical is one of reduction of the many-into-one manifestation and the single essence. As a poet, Kambar can only be plural and hence rich. Behind all the Upanishadic monism, India is mythical. Because we still bargain with our gods and walk among them and sometimes as them, our worship is essentially participatory, rituals in which men and their gods are parts of the same structure. In this, we Indians are a mythical people. To be a poet, Kambar needs to be mythical.

Kambar writes at a time when a version of Western modernism is the presiding tone in Kannada literature. Indeed, some of his less important writings show a naive anxiety to be 'contemporary'. However, in his more important works, he seems to question the validity of whether Western structures of modernism are necessary to the writer's task of relating to his environment. To Kambar, the problem of being is more fundamental and universal. Modernism simply does not suffice. Kambar's work is a process of acceptance and transformation. Modernism is one of precise rejection.

The writer always deals with the sense of time and the sense of space. Kambar draws his texture of experience mainly from his sense of space, it forms the core of his writing. He is even a bit suspicious of an insistence on time, for time is abstract and could grow to be a neurosis in a writer. To a writer like Kambar, as to the painter and to the sculptor, place is the core of perception. Kambar certainly is of his time, as unavoidably as he is of his place; but the relative emphasis decides the character of his writing and keeps it apart from that of his peers in Kannada. Environment to him is the sense of place, ranging from the actual to the fantastic–mythical.

Kambar's insistent relationship with place also has something to do with his social background. He does not belong to an upper, or Sanskritized, caste. Hence, he is distant from the contrasts central to the upper-caste inheritance: time–eternity, janma–moksha, appearance–essence and so on, all of which are dwelt on in the traditional Upanishadic culture. Not being burdened with these essentially time-based structures, he is with a child's 'illiterate' fascination for powerful immediacies of sense. A true and easy sense of the many is his kind of relating: hence his inevitable kinship with myth-making.

In this country, with its variety of social and intellectual structures, from the heavily abstracting Sanatana to the non-reducing sensibility of the primitive and oppressed, it is possible to relate to one's environment with a power and variety unthinkable in the urbanized and anonymous social structure elsewhere. A mythical episteme is still valid, natural and real here. To say this is to point out the core of Kambar's importance to literature.

Rajiv Taranath
1989

A NOTE ON *JOKUMARASWAMI*

Jokumaraswami is a phallic god and he is worshipped even today in the villages of north Karnataka. The annual festival which usually occurs in August–September, Jokumara Hunnive (full-moon night), is named after him. The worship starts on the eighth day (ashtami) of the month of Bhadrapada. Women belonging to the castes of fisherman, washerman and lime-maker make phallus-shaped idols of Jokumaraswami out of wet clay. Applying butter to the phallus tip, they place the idols in baskets. Packing each idol firmly into an erect position with neem leaves, they carry the baskets on their heads and go from house to house, singing songs in praise of Jokumaraswami. Householders give them alms of salt, chillies and tamarind.

In some villages, the village boys get together and make a huge phallus, eight to ten feet long, and tip it with lime. At its base, they stick hair gathered from a barber shop. It is believed that barren women become fertile if they sit on this phallus. In other villages, they cook snake gourd as an embodiment of Jokumaraswami and feed it to the husbands of barren women.

Jokumaraswami is associated with rain. It is believed that even a rainless month will end with a shower on Jokumara Hunnive. There are many stories about Jokumaraswami in folklore. There is an ancient myth behind all these stories, a myth which is relevant to the play. It goes somewhat like this: Jokumaraswami, the son of Shiva, takes birth on earth as the son of Ditnadevi. From the second day after his birth till the sixth, he seduces all the women of the village. On the seventh day, the angry cuckolds of the village kill him with ritual cruelty. Wherever his bloods falls, the earth turns green and fertile.

Jokumaraswami was first produced in the original Kannada by Pratima Nataka Ranga, at the open-air theatre of Ravindra Kalakshetra, Bangalore, on 11 May 1972 with the following cast:

GOWDA	Girish Karnad
BASANNA	Umesh Rudra
GURYA	Krishna Raju
GOWDATHI	Sarada Umesh Rudra
NINGI	Revati
SHARI	Girija
BASSI	Kalpana
SHIVI	Asha
SERVANTS	1. Prasanna
	2. Arjuna
	3. Mohan Ram
	4. Gopalakrishna
SUTRADHARA	Chandrasekhar Kambar
HIMMELA	B. V. Karanth
MELA (CHORUS)	Siddharamaiah, Bharathi, Doddarange Gauda, Sunanda, Vijayalakshmi

DIRECTION	B. V. Karanth
MUSIC	Chandrasekhar Kambar
STAGE DESIGN	V. Ramamurthy
COSTUMES	Prema Karanth

The Hindi version of this play was produced by Theatre Unit and Avishkar, and directed by Satyadev Dubey, at the Prithvi Theatre, Bombay, on 20 June 1979. It was also produced and directed by Rajinder Nath at Shriram Centre for Art and Culture, New Delhi, on 17 March 1980.

Jokumaraswami has also been translated into and produced in Punjabi, Tamil and Gujarati. It has been performed at Calcutta, Chandigarh, Madras and Ahmedabad, among other places.

GANNA PADA

(Opening Prayer)

We salute you, O Lords and Masters!
Don't please disturb the play.

Young novices we are, frightened of paint,
Do attend well to our ballad.

Sit through it, O men and women,
And let the hall be full,
And let the love of wise men
Be upon us.

Lord Savalagi Shivalinga,
May your blessings be upon us.

PROLOGUE

At the centre of the stage, there is a basket filled with vegetables. In the middle of this basket, a snake gourd stands prominently.

SUTRADHARA. Salutations to all of you, sitting or standing. Can you see this new god? His name is Jokumaraswami. Not that he is new to you. But there is a difference between him and other gods. The other gods grant a mouthful of boons the moment they are flattered a little. But somehow or other, like the promises our ministers make, not one boon comes true. On the other hand, this god does not speak when he is flattered. But if you hold him in your arms after worship, he fills your lap with children. Indeed, the theme of this evening's play is the story of this unusual god. Who's there? Ho! Himmela!

HIMMELA. What? Why did you call me?

SUTRADHARA. Jokumaraswami must be worshipped before the commencement of our play. Please bring all the necessary ingredients and offer him worship according to the scriptures.

HIMMELA. Where did you say the god was?

SUTRADHARA. Can't you see him there?

HIMMELA. Ah, you mean this god!

SUTRADHARA. Why, what's wrong with this god?

HIMMELA. Instead of worshipping Ganesha at the commencement of the play, you want to worship this kind of god. Don't you understand? What will those who know think about us?

SUTRADHARA. You idiot! When all gods are one and the same, what does it matter which god you worship? Come to think of it, this Jokumaraswami is the younger brother of Ganesha, and indeed today's play is about him. You shouldn't forget our original god.

HIMMELA. What's so great about Him?

SUTRADHARA. On this auspicious occasion, if barren women offer worship to this god, and afterwards make a curry out of him to feed their husbands, dozens of children will be born in a jiffy.

HIMMELA. Quite right. And that's why a few women have come to the show. You don't seem to know anything about family planning at all.

SUTRADHARA. My dear Himmela, if young women who have lost the love of their husbands, simply cook and feed this god to them, then all wayward husbands will begin to stick to their homes like ageing pet dogs.

HIMMELA. I suppose many women don't know this.

SUTRADHARA. Don't chatter any more about such a god. Go fetch the ingredients for worship.

HIMMELA. All right, all right. 'Bring', you order, so I'll bring. But later, if people scoff and scold, it's your look-out. Shall I bring?

SUTRADHARA. Yes.

HIMMELA. You are shameless. What shall I bring?

SUTRADHARA. Holy grass, holy leaves.

HIMMELA. Holy grass and leaves? Is your god some cow? Why don't you let him graze in a field?

SUTRADHARA. You idiot! Don't talk lightly about a god who's like fire. Cleanse yourself and bring the holy leaves.

HIMMELA. So be it, Sutradhara. Here are holy leaves and holy grass.

SUTRADHARA. And get some rosewater too, all right?

HIMMELA. Yes, I've understood.

SUTRADHARA. What did you understand?

HIMMELA. The water barbers use for shaving, isn't that rosewater?

SUTRADHARA. You idiot! Purified water is called rosewater. Get that rosewater.

HIMMELA. Yes. Here, I've brought it.

SUTRADHARA. Get some flowers and fruits, and, to offer worship, a chaste woman.

HIMMELA. Your god seems to be terribly expensive. I can bring flowers, I can bring fruits, but where will I find a pure, chaste woman? You're sure you want only a pure, chaste woman?

SUTRADHARA. Yes, only a pure, chaste woman will do.

HIMMELA. And if there's a little adulteration?

SUTRADHARA. Shut up.

HIMMELA. Sutradhara, I can get you fruit and flowers. But I can't manage this chaste-woman business. There simply isn't anyone of that sort these days. If you want, you can count me in as a chaste woman, and make do with me.

SUTRADHARA. Why, what's wrong? Why do you say this?

HIMMELA. Why? Will any self-respecting person come to worship such a god? In fact, if you want to know the truth, if you're looking for anyone who is at all chaste, you will find him among us four or five boys. Tell me, why is this god always after women?

SUTRADHARA. All right, you do the worship.

Sutradhara sings with the chorus, Mela, while Himmela performs the act of worship.

MELA. Come, my little lord,
Come, my pretty moon,
Come, Jokumaraswami!
Lord of the green and lord of abuse,
Lord of spicy offerings.
You fell as rain and sprouted as harvest,
And laughed young and fresh among the wild flowers.
You laid all the girls within two days of your birth.
And their men came chasing you with their sickles.

HIMMELA. How can you worship such an obscene god especially in a public place?

SUTRADHARA. Such labels are for human beings. Among the gods, there's no 'clean' or 'obscene'.

HIMMELA. Do you know what you have forgotten at the moment?

SUTRADHARA. What?

HIMMELA. You have forgotten shame.

SUTRADHARA. If I hold on to shame, my god will get angry. Listen quietly.

HIMMELA. Right, shoot!

MELA. Menstruating maidens you laid
On the third day after your birth,
And the uncles chased you
With axes and sticks.
The old women you pulled, lord,
On the fourth day,
And the old men chased you

With rocks.
The wives you pulled, lord,
On the fifth day
And their children chased you
With net and rope.
The widows you tugged,
On the sixth day
And they set
Five hundred on you.

HIMMELA. Given the slightest of chances, you're in great voice, what do you think? Who doesn't know how to yell out a song? Shall I? (*He sings*)

You sat in a car and fell into the theatre.
Don't you have a home to sleep in?

SUTRADHARA. Why? Didn't I sing beautifully?

HIMMELA. Oh yes! Too beautifully. Do please sing a little less beautifully. Otherwise, the people gathered here might understand you. The point is to sing it un-understandably.

SUTRADHARA. All right. Shall I then describe the greatness of this god in prose?

HIMMELA. Yes please. Or else this god is a big risk.

SUTRADHARA. In which case, listen. This our great god, the god of green, of rains, of harvests, of abuses, Jokumaraswami . . .

HIMMELA. Oho!

SUTRADHARA. Within two days of his birth, all the girls in the town . . .

HIMMELA. Aha!

SUTRADHARA. He laid.

HIMMELA. You went wrong there.

SUTRADHARA. Why?

HIMMELA. What a rare creature this god of yours is! Only men who're idle chase and lay women. And your god acts like them. He laid girls, he laid hags, shouldn't you at least be more prudent in your language?

SUTRADHARA. How?

HIMMELA. I mean the term 'laid'. People here think it's obscene. Do you see who is sitting in front? You really can't be obscene in such a gathering. Shall I tell you a trick? Instead of saying he 'laid' them, say he 'made love to them', he 'made love to them'.

SUTRADHARA. Righto! This is our great god . . .

HIMMELA. . . . green god, that god, this god, etc., god . . . Proceed.

SUTRADHARA. You know what he did on the third day after his birth?

HIMMELA. What?

SUTRADHARA. All those who menstruated . . .

HIMMELA. Obscene again! Remove that word, and say girls who had 'come of age.'

SUTRADHARA. On the third day of his birth, all the girls who had come of age . . .

HIMMELA. . . . he made love to them.

SUTRADHARA. On the fourth day, all the hags . . .

HIMMELA. . . . made love . . .

SUTRADHARA. On the fifth day, the wives . . .

HIMMELA. . . . made love . . .

SUTRADHARA. On the sixth day, the widows . . .

HIMMELA. . . . made love. Sutradhara, are you cooking this up or is it true? Anyway, what happened then?

SUTRADHARA. And then, on the seventh day, the husbands of the wives came with axes. The old women's old men came with rocks, and the sons of widows came with ropes and nets. In all, five hundred of them. And where did they come to?

HIMMELA. They came to Jokumaraswami.

SUTRADHARA. And what did they do?

HIMMELA. Wait a moment. I think you should describe what happened in poetry. Prose might be a bit dangerous.

SUTRADHARA. If so, then listen. What did the five hundred do to Jokumaraswami?

HIMMELA. What?

MELA. Count, and they are five hundred.
Count, and the hands are a thousand
Which grip and chop the tender god.
A thousand hands. In each hand
A sickle or an axe,
Which slash to death the tender god.
Killed and thrown him,
They have slashed and thrown him,
And the flowing blood
Fills the river and the pond.
Where the blood falls, springs the sprout
And the shoot,
and all the earth is fresh, is green.

During the song, untouchable Shari enters dancing and, after bowing, is about to carry away the sacred basket. Himmela notices her.

HIMMELA. Not bad, your god. He's got a luscious customer. (*Running to her*) Who art thou, beauteous damsel? Why hast thou come out of thy noble palace to this noble gathering? Art thou about to carry away this god? By what name art thou known? Be good enough to tell.

SHARI. What is this? You talk like a book.

HIMMELA. Sutradhara, please come here. I can't manage.

SUTRADHARA. Lady, who are you? What's your name? Tell us prettily.

SHARI. Sutradhara, do I have to tell you?

SUTRADHARA. Yes, you must.

SHARI. Sutradhara, old men call me little girl, little girl. Small boys call me old woman. Gentleman who are neither call me the untouchable whore Shari.

SUTRADHARA. Lady, now we know that your name is Sharavva, and the people gathered here also know it. But why did you come here and why do you desire to carry away Jokumaraswami? Please do let us know.

SHARI. Sutradhara, Jokumaraswami is a great god. He gives children to barren women, and husbands to maidens.

HIMMELA. Yes, and he gives you clients.

SHARI. I waited to see if some barren woman would carry away our god. None came. At least let me take him. As I get older, I get fewer clients. I could at least hold the few I have if I feed them with a curry made of my god.

HIMMELA. So, it seems this god is really useful.

SUTRADHARA. Sharavva, if that's the case, please take the god.

Shari picks up the basket.

HIMMELA. Here, wait, wait. (*He runs to stand behind her in a traditional pose of bestowing a blessing*) My son, Sutradhara, I'm pleased with your worship. I bless this evening's play. Begin your play hereafter.

Sutradhara bows.

MUSKET GOD

MELA. There is a Gowda in a certain place,
And the Gowda is a rogue,
And he wears a big paunch,
And he struts about carrying a gun.
Lord of the town and its boundary,
Gold, silver and gold again,
And pretty wench and girl,
All, claims the Gowda, are his.
The Gowda has a wife,
Let's call her Gowdathi,
A comely woman she is.
Rapt, she watches
The parrot flying.

As the song ends, Gowda enters grandly from amid the audience, followed by four men carrying a musket, who are dancing and singing, 'This is our god, Dum Dum is his name.'

SUTRADHARA. O thou brave man who hast entered here along with this retinue, who art thou? What is thy name? Please narrate all prettily.

Gowda looks at the four members of his retinue, and, gesturing to them to answer the Sutradhara, he sits on a string bed. The four men bring the musket, stand it in front of the Sutradhara and, hanging a turban on its barrel, laugh among themselves.

ONE. If you want to know who this is . . .

ALL. This is our god,
Dum Dum is his name.

SUTRADHARA. Is his name Dum Dum? The audience is anxious—what does this god do? Please describe in detail.

ONE. He has a trigger and behind the trigger a bolt. The moment he takes aim, he jumps once. 'Dum!' and that's the end. So great is our god.

ALL. This is our god,
Dum Dum is his name.

TWO. In a war, the soldiers shoot at corpses. But our god fires only at healthy people. One day, he fired at a sick man. Where was that?

THREE. In the devil's field.

FOUR. Yes, in the devil's field. And as he fired at the sick man, our god didn't jump, didn't sing, didn't say 'Dum!' He didn't speak for three days altogether. Then, one day, twelve untouchable field labourers were stood in a line and our god fired at them saying, 'Dum.' Can you tell me what remained?

SUTRADHARA. A dozen corpses!

TWO. No! When others fire, there are corpses. When our Dum Dum god fires, there's only ash and a whiff of smoke. How can I praise our god!

ALL. This is our god,
Dum Dum is his name.

SUTRADHARA. Yes, and what does your god look like?

THREE. Our god Dum Dum has a big belly. He digests anything. Fellows like you get the gripes after eating two or three rotis. Our god can digest human flesh, and he just loves chicks.

ALL. This is our god,
Dum Dum is his name.

GOWDA. Hello Sutradhara. Do you know who I am?

SUTRADHARA. Sir, I now know who you are, and so do the socialists gathered here. (*Pointing at Basanna who has entered quietly in the meanwhile*) Who's he? And why does he stand there?

ONE. This is the food of our Dum Dum god.

TWO. No. He's the lamb meant for our Dum Dum god.

THREE. No. He's the milch cow of our god.

GOWDATHI (*entering from the wings*). Listen.

GOWDA. Why do you come here in front of all these people? Go in, I'll listen to you later.

FOUR (*pointing out to the Gowdathi*). That's the field of Dum Dum god.

Gowdathi goes in.

SUTRADHARA. Doesn't this fellow have a name?

ONE. I wonder.

BASANNA. Basanna.

Gowda gets up immediately.

GOWDA. Basanna? Come, come Basanna. You all there, go away and come back later. Basanna, why do you keep standing outside? Come in, come in. Would you care for a smoke?

(*The four move to one side of the stage and Sutradhara joins Mela.*)

I know you are very cut up about your father's death. You shouldn't think I'm not sad about it. What a lovely old man, your father. Every morning he used to come calling on me and borrow a bidi[1] from me. But what's to be done? The old man was very obstinate, and wouldn't

1 A popular, inexpensive 'cigarette' made of rolled leaf and tobacco.

listen to anybody. I myself told him, as to a parrot, not to sleep in that field, that there was a ghost there, the ghost of a woman who had seven children. Did he listen to me? No. He snubbed me, saying that even evil spirits are better than some human beings. And he went to the field. Next morning, when I went to meet him, there he was . . . Sit down. Don't keep standing. You shouldn't worry too much. You can stay in my house.

BASANNA. I know how my father died.

GOWDA. Not just you, the whole village knows. The earth of that field is very unkind. Why, only yesterday, Gurya's two lambs were lost there.

BASANNA. I know how my father died.

GOWDA. Are you crazy? You seem to suspect me. You know why? You've taken all this too much to heart. That's why. Come, have a smoke and you'll feel better.

BASANNA. Gowda, let me tell you something loud and clear. I know how my father died. I know how he carved a field from out of a forest. I know how I shall never give up that field.

GOWDA. Since you know so much, do you also know that your father had borrowed money?

BASANNA. Whichever way you look at it, it was only 200 rupees. For twenty years, he gave you half his produce every year, and the loan is still not repaid?

GOWDA. Let that pass. Do you know in whose name that field is registered?

BASANNA. I don't know all that—the field is mine, and I'm going to plough it. If you have anything more to say, tell it to my back.

GOWDA. In that case, I don't understand what you say. Say all that to my gun.

Basanna kicks the gun and goes away. Gowdathi enters and speaks after Basanna has left.

GOWDATHI. Please listen!

The servants approach when they see Gurya coming from a distance. Gowdathi goes in.

ONE. My lord, Gurya has come and is waiting outside.

GOWDA. Bring him in. (*Gurya comes in, frightened*) Come, Gurya . . . This lamb is frightened, go away, you.

The four servants move away.

GURYA. My lord, two of my lambs were killed and eaten by the servants.

GOWDA. Whose servants?

GURYA. Your servants, the ones standing there.

GOWDA. You bastard, you wag your tongue too much. Why did you allow your sheep to graze there? Didn't you let them graze in the devil's field?

GURYA. Yes.

GOWDA. You let them graze there, and the devil killed them. And you have the cheek to blame my servants. You bastard! The devil broke even a man like Basanna's father, will it leave your sheep alone? To add to this, you spread the scandal throughout the village. If anything dies in the village, it is said that Gowda or his servants are responsible. Bastards! You don't seem to appreciate the value of a Gowda. Wait a moment and I'll tell you who killed . . . (*He takes up the gun.*)

GURYA. Not me, sir! Basanna said all this.

GOWDA. Basanna? Tell me the truth. Why have you come here?

GURYA (*not knowing what to say*). Nothing special, my lord, I came here . . . to press your feet.

GOWDA. Well, press them, then.

Gurya starts pressing Gowda's feet, in great fear.

GOWDA. Gurya, you bastard, do you know who I am?

GURYA. You are the Gowda of the village.

GOWDA. Do you know who you are?

GURYA. Your slave, my lord.

GOWDA. Are you frightened?

GURYA. No, my lord.

GOWDA. Are you afraid of Basanna?

GURYA. No, my lord.

GOWDA. Not frightened of me or of Basanna? You've become quite a politician.

GURYA. I'm frightened only of you.

GOWDA. If you fear me, then why did you go to Basanna? Bark!

GURYA. I'll bark, my lord.

GOWDA. Why did you go to Basanna?

GURYA. I didn't.

GOWDA. He came to you?

GURYA. Yes.

GOWDA. What did you say? What did he say? Tell me everything properly, or else, you bastard, I'll skin you alive.

GURYA. Basanna said, 'Gurya, I hear you've sold your field to the Gowda?'

I said, 'No, we owed Gowda some money. He took the field in part repayment.'

Basanna said, 'How much?'

I said, '300.'

He said, 'How could you sell him five acres for a mere 300 rupees?'

I said, 'I don't know.'

GOWDA. You son of a dog, you don't know? How long is it since I gave you 300 rupees?

GURYA. Three or four years.

GOWDA. Three or four years? Shall I get the papers? Ten years. Ten.

GURYA. I was a small child then.

GOWDA. When you were young, did you eat rice or cow dung? Do the documents lie? Does your thumb print lie? Didn't you take the money at the Durgavva's fair on Amavasya[2]?

GURYA. Yes, it was on Amavasya night.

The four servants in the background stand up and move closer.

GOWDA. How long is it since that Amavasya?

GURYA. Ten years.

GOWDA. What is the total of the principal and the interest for ten years?

GURYA. Five acres, my lord.

The four move away again.

GOWDA. It is ten, not five. Bastard! I've let you keep on working for me only because I pity you. Isn't there any value for a Gowda who rules the earth? If I so wish, I can make not only you but even Basanna eat dirt, understand?

GURYA. Yes, I understand.

GOWDA. Gurya, what do you understand?

2 In Hinduism, the day of the new moon.

GURYA. That he'll eat dirt.

GOWDA. Go tell Basanna his father hasn't given me last year's share. He's not to step into the field without repaying the loan.

GURYA. All right.

GOWDA. When will you go?

GURYA. Right now, sir.

GOWDA. Press my feet now. Go later.

Shivi and Bassi enter, but go inside hurriedly when they see Gowda. Then Ningi enters and removes her slippers.

GOWDA. Who is this bird, Gurya? Hey, you, stop! (*Ningi covers her face with her sari and stops*) Whose daughter are you?

GURYA. She is Gurupada's daughter.

GOWDA. She's come of age, see how ripe she is. Isn't she married yet?

GURYA. Not yet, sir.

GOWDA. What's your name, girl?

GURYA. Gowda is asking you, tell him. When Gowda himself wants to know your name why don't you reply?

GOWDA. Maybe she is scared! What a mouth-watering bit of a girl she is! Are you scared?

NINGI (*letting her sari slip*). You are not a tiger or a bear for me to be scared of. I'm not panting with my tongue out just because the village Gowda asked my name . . . yaah . . . (*She sticks her tongue out at him.*)

GOWDA. You crazy girl, who do you think you're speaking to? Can't you see clearly?

NINGI. Of course I can. The sun is shining and I have two eyes. Shall I say it? This is Gowda's face, these are my slippers. (*She prepares to leave.*)

GOWDA. Stop, girl. Tell your father this. Tell him that I haven't left any land in this village untouched.

NINGI. There's plenty of land in this village where even the sun's rays haven't fallen. Understand?

She exits quickly.

GOWDA. To come to my place and give me such cheek! The chick has flown away. Gurya . . .

GURYA. Sir?

GOWDA. Will you marry her?

GURYA. Sir . . .

GOWDA. Will you marry her?

GURYA. Heh, heh, heh . . .

GOWDA. I'll sell her for three rupees. Will you buy?

GURYA. Heh, heh, heh . . .

GOWDA. Go cook a curry with plenty of spice. You eat it in my name, if you can't give it to me. What do you say?

GURYA. Heh, heh, heh . . .

GOWDA. Stop cackling, you bastard. Which girl will fall for a cur like you? How old are you?

GURYA. Twenty-five.

GOWDA. Have you ever seen a woman's thighs?

GURYA. No, sir.

GOWDA. How can you understand? Gurya, I want to catch this jungle fowl.

GURYA. I know how to catch one, my lord.

GOWDA. Really? Tell me how.

GURYA. You should put a cockerel in a cage. You should hang the cage in the forest. And when you crow like a cock, ko ko ko, wild hens will turn up. Shoot them.

GOWDA. At least you know this much.

GURYA. But even when a true cock like you crowed, the bird slipped away.

GOWDA. Shut up, you bastard. Come here. Hold your ears. (*Gurya does as he says*) Sit down, get up, down, up . . . Press my leg. (*Gurya starts pressing his leg*) Gurya, to whom do the villagers pay more respect? To me or to Basanna?

GURYA. To you, sir.

GOWDA. Who are they more scared of?

GURYA. You, sir.

GOWDA. Say it properly.

GURYA. The men are scared of you, the women are scared of Basanna.

GOWDA. Really? Which woman has not been touched by Basanna?

GURYA. The one who was here just now.

GOWDA. Oh? What does she call Basanna?

GURYA. She calls him brother.

GOWDA. Is that so? She'll call me uncle. Tell Gurupada . . .

GURYA. Yes sir . . .

GOWDA. What'll you tell him?

GURYA. I'll tell him that Gowda is hungry, give him your bird to eat.

GOWDA. Go. I'll follow you shortly.

Gurya leaves. Gowdathi comes in as Gowda is picking up the gun.

GOWDATHI. What, are you going somewhere?

GOWDA. You have the nerve to ask me! Haven't I told you not to ask where and why I'm going out?

GOWDATHI. Will you at least come home tonight?

GOWDA. She is worried as if she can't bear to part from me. Finish telling me whatever you want to say while I smoke a bidi. I'll listen. (*He lights the bidi.*)

GOWDATHI. Tonight is Jokumara's full-moon night. It has been ten years since we got married.

GOWDA. So?

GOWDATHI. On that day, the full moon was so big.

GOWDA. So it was.

GOWDATHI. On that day, my mother said that by next Jokumara full-moon night, a little male child would be playing in our house.

GOWDA. Really? I don't remember.

GOWDATHI. I had a dream last night.

GOWDA. Did you? What did you dream?

GOWDATHI. There was a full moon. A rainbow-coloured parrot was sitting on a tree in our garden. Even in the moonlight its colours were shining. Then, for some reason, everyone started laughing. Up there, our moon was growing smaller and smaller like a rusted coin . . . Why have you neglected me so much?

GOWDA. Either you are still sleepy, or you must have fever. I've told you not to worry too much. If I worried like you, I wouldn't have so much hair left on my head.

GOWDATHI. How can you understand a woman's needs?

GOWDA. Come on, then, make me understand. Here, I'll light another bidi. Tell me.

GOWDATHI. As if you really care for what I say. There was an old man hiding behind that small moon, taking aim at the parrot . . .

GOWDA. You're still dreaming. Wake up.

GOWDATHI. We've been married for ten years. Have I ever asked you a favour?

GOWDA. What do you lack? First tell me that.

GOWDATHI. I have everything! Food to eat, clothes to wear . . . Do you know what Gurupada's daughter said?

GOWDA. What?

GOWDATHI. 'You have a field as big as the forest, a house as big as the village, but there is no child in the house.'

GOWDA. Did she say that? Must do something about it.

GOWDATHI. You said the same thing when we got married!

GOWDA. Really? I don't remember. Tell her I won't forget this time.

GOWDATHI. Tonight is Jokumaraswami's full-moon night. I believe that if we worship Jokumaraswami and then cook and eat him, we will have children. So please come home for dinner.

GOWDA. Oho! So that's why the ladies are here?

GOWDATHI. Yes.

GOWDA. Has Gurupada's daughter also come here for the same reason?

GOWDATHI. Yes. It seems you said something to her and she went home.

GOWDA. Yes. What did you say her name was?

GOWDATHI. Ningi.

GOWDA. OK. So I'll come home for dinner this evening.

GOWDATHI. Will you see if you can get a parrot?

GOWDA. Will you do one thing?

GOWDATHI. Why one? Give me ten things to do.

GOWDA. Not ten, one is enough. Will you do it?

GOWDATHI. Tell me what.

GOWDA. Will you shut up and go inside?

He goes out. Mela sings, 'This is our god, Dum Dum is his name.'

RISE AND COME, BELOVED PARROT

MELA (*sings*). Rise and come to us, beloved parrot, relishing the eastern breeze and filled with moonlight.

Bring to the parched earth the season of blossoming flowers,
O, bird of distant lands.
Hearts are filled with sand, nests droop from the gaunt tree, the young in the womb cry, disconsolate even early in the night.
Anxious I stand. Come.

Gowdathi is on the veranda. Bassi is in the kitchen inside. Bassi speaks from within.

GOWDATHI. Bassi . . .

BASSI. I'm coming, ma'am.

GOWDATHI. Come quick . . .

BASSI. I just have to wipe my hands.

GOWDATHI. You still have to sweep the floor and wash the threshold.

BASSI (*comes out*). Have you had a bath?

GOWDATHI. Doesn't it look as if I've had one? Whatever I do, it's the same. I feel thirsty from head to toe. Everything should be ready before Gowda returns. What have you told Shivi?

BASSI. I've asked her to get Jokumaraswami from Sutradhara's basket.

During the following conversation, Bassi sweeps, draws auspicious patterns on the floor and lights the oven. Gowdathi helps her now and then.

GOWDATHI. Bassi . . .

BASSI. Yes, ma'am.

GOWDATHI. Will I have children if this worship is done properly?

BASSI. Would I lie, ma'am? Do you know that Deviri down the road?

GOWDATHI. The one who got married on the same day as I did?

BASSI. The same Deviri.

GOWDATHI. But she has children.

BASSI. That's right, and it's a long story. She didn't have children for a long time, like you. Her husband was ready to marry again. They even saw some prospective brides. One day, Deviri was crying into her sari in the fields. 'Why are you crying?' I asked her. 'What can I say? My husband wants to marry again. God hasn't given me any children,' she said. Whatever you may say ma'am, don't I know who is barren and who is a mother? She smelt like a newly ploughed field even at a distance.

GOWDATHI. There's a season to everything. It's not right to cross its limit.

BASSI. Gowda's conduct is just not right. What's the use of having fields all round the village? Who will he leave it all to when he dies? Is he bothered? A young woman like you is sitting at home worrying about it, and he'd rather see a prostitute's thighs than his wife's face.

GOWDATHI. It's all fate.

BASSI. Ma'am. Why do you make me say these things? If the balls don't bless, what can god's blessings do? It needs a strong man to fulfil a woman. It's not enough to boast and threaten. Look at my husband. Years since we married, and he hasn't thrashed me even once. Still, if I see him coming, I start trembling like a creeper in the breeze. It's true, ma'am, even old hags conceive if they so much as cross my husband's piss.

GOWDATHI. It's all the grace of god. I prayed to god and he has thrown a broom in my lap.

BASSI. Why do you upset yourself so? My name is not Bassi if this worship misfires.

GOWDATHI. By the way, what did you tell Deviri?

BASSI. Oh yes! Deviri was crying—I asked her why. She said, 'What can I say? My husband is bringing home another wife.' 'Why is he bringing another wife?' 'Because I'm barren,' she said, and started weeping again. And yet, if men approach Deviri, her eyes start dancing like a leaf on a creeper. I've seen this myself. How can I believe that she's barren?

GOWDATHI. I have told him so many times that this house needs children. He says, 'You're tired, go and rest.' Even other children are scared to come here. The other day, I offered them sweets. But did even one wretched child so much as turn this way? I wept inside when I saw them running away. 'What is this woman's life, god?' I cried. How can my cry reach god? His heart must be made of stone.

BASSI. Look here, ma'am. Call me a wretch if you want, but a home should be lively with the sound of children and children should be weeping and their mother should be threatening them with the very devil. How charming it all sounds! And here? At night, this house has only one lamp flickering, as if about to be put out any minute. There don't seem to be people in the house at all, and if there are, they speak in whispers.

GOWDATHI. What did you tell Deviri?

BASSI. I told her not to worry and to worship Jokumaraswami. She worshipped him, cooked him and fed him to her husband. The moment he ate that, he started chasing Deviri like one demented. He was always inside her. Do you know what happened next? A child on Wednesday, a child on Saturday. It was as easy as laying eggs!

GOWDATHI. So even she got children from Jokumaraswami?

BASSI. Jokumaraswami is not a god to be taken lightly, ma'am.

GOWDATHI. Bassi, does anyone here have a pet parrot?

BASSI. Hah! A parrot. Do you know Basanna? He has a parrot, a very beautiful one. It doesn't fly away even if it's let out of its cage—it's always on his shoulder.

GOWDATHI. Really?

BASSI. Ma'am, he's even taught it to speak. It lisps so adorably!

GOWDATHI. Is that really true?

BASSI. It's true all right. All the village girls speak to it when they go to collect water.

Shivi enters.

SHIVI. Ma'am, everything is ruined.

GOWDATHI. Why?

SHIVI. That prostitute Shari beat us to it. She's taken Jokumaraswami from Sutradhara.

GOWDATHI. Then why didn't you go to her place?

SHIVI. How can I go to where the untouchables live?

GOWDATHI. For my sake, go. How can I spend another year mumbling god's name in vain? Go, and I'll give you loads of gifts.

SHIVI. How can a respectably married woman go to a whore's house, ma'am?

GOWDATHI. Right. As they say, you can't go to heaven unless you yourself die. Stay here, I'll be back.

Music. Gowdathi exits.

BIRD OF THE SEASON

Gowdathi enters, sweeping the veranda of the whore Shari's house with the end of her sari.

GOWDATHI. Beloved whore,
Whore, my mother,
Are you home?
Barren I come
To entreat you.
Pity you have none.
With my sari end
I sweep your front yard.
I stand, my lap barren.
Come out, I beg you,
And meet me.

SHARI. Who are you, sweeping the veranda of a whore's house?
Who are you, O friend,
Why have you come?
Why do you sweep?
A rich family, a virtuous one,
You seem to belong to.
Why do you, O well-married one,
Come to a mere whore's yard?
Madam, you appear to be well-married and beautiful.
Who are you? Kindly be so good as to tell me.

GOWDATHI. Mother . . .

SHARI. You should call a low whore like me 'bitch', not 'mother'. Who may you be?

GOWDATHI. Like you, I'm a woman.

SHARI. I know that. I could call you an elder or younger sister. You look married. Tell me your name.

GOWDATHI. The bird of the season has come and sat in your house. I'll tell you my name if you give me that bird.

SHARI. Why, madam, do you talk in riddles? Why do you tire me out without giving me your name? What and where is this bird of the season?

GOWDATHI. You have it at home and yet you ask me where it is.

SHARI. Don't kill me with riddles. My house is blessed by your coming. Tell me your name and why you are here.

GOWDATHI. Mother, I'll tell you my name if you give me Jokumaraswami.

SHARI. What rival are you,
What whore are you?
Want me to die, do you?
To the grave should I go,
No food, no water,
Not even a client!
I sit here waiting
And you pretend
To sweep my yard.
What whore are you,
What rival are you?
Of Jokumaraswami I wanted to
Cook a dish

And feed all the town males
And hold them in my sari
And lay them at my threshold
And you come to sweep my yard.
What rival are you,
What whore are you?
Twenty years have passed
Since I, a whore became—
Nothing earned, nothing saved.
I thought that by the mercy of
Jokumaraswami I could purchase
Rope to hang my wretched self!
And you come to sweep my yard.
What rival are you,
What whore are you?
Which town whore,
Which lane whore?

GOWDATHI. Mother,
Spreading my sari I beg,
Your feet I clasp,
Show me mercy!

SHARI. You fool, which female will let go of Jokumaraswami? I'm getting old. I don't have a daughter like you to look after me. This body of mine has never slept without perfumed oil in its hair and a lover by its side. Now I've got a spell to bring all the lovers to me. How can I give that to you? No, I won't.

GOWDATHI. Do not, I beg of you,
Refuse me.

As your daughter,
Fill my lap.
Spreading my sari I beg,
Your feet I clasp,
Show me mercy.

SHARI. If I had a soft heart, would I be a whore? How can I give away such a stroke of luck to some wayfarer?

GOWDATHI. Wretched and barren,
I do entreat,
Spreading my sari I beg,
Your feet I clasp,
Show me mercy.

SHARI. I feel sad that you are barren. But what can I do? How can I let go of the good fortune in my hands? Go, after telling me your name?

GOWDATHI. The wife of the Gowda.
I am Gowdathi.
Still, I implore,
Show me mercy.

SHARI. The village Gowdathi? How can you be so mad, madam? You put aside your status and come to a whore's house begging! Have you been married long?

GOWDATHI. It is ten years today since I married.

SHARI. Don't you know Gowda's weakness yet? Even if I give you Jokumaraswami, how can you get children from Gowda?

GOWDATHI. Why not? So many have borne children to Jokumaraswami!

SHARI. Yes, others may have, but you still don't know Gowda's nature. Except for a vain desire to claim everything in this world as his, what else does he have? Look at me. I've spent a lifetime rubbing myself against hot men. Shall I tell you my experience? Look at Basanna. Any girl he looks at gets wet. He makes them wet even in their dreams. But the same girls have a hard time hiding their giggles when they see Gowda. Can such a fellow have children? On the day I had my first period, Gowda came to ceremonially break my seal. He gave me a bag of rice, a sari, a blouse and five rupees. What wouldn't a young whore give to have Gowda as her first client? When I entered the bedroom with my sari loosened . . . Gowda was snoring. I spent the night pressing his feet. He went away in the morning as if nothing had happened. Since that day he has broken the seals of ten or fifteen girl whores and when you ask them how, they say what I've just said. You know why he did this?

GOWDATHI. He must've felt bad about coming to a whorehouse.

SHARI. Every day you press his feet and scrub his back in the bath. You have seen his front and you have seen his back and you still insist on loving him. You are a proper wife indeed. Do you know why he did what he did? Whether he lay with them or not, the children of all the whores whose seals he was supposed to have broken would be counted as his children. So Gowda addresses anybody in the village as 'son of mine' . . . Can such a Gowda give you children?

GOWDATHI. Why not, with the blessings of Jokumaraswami?

SHARI. Do please take Jokumaraswami! But now that you have stood at the threshold of a whore's house, at least learn to have your wits about you.

GOWDATHI. Mother, how can I ever repay this great favour? Just bless me by saying once that I'll have children.

SHARI. Go, you'll have children.

She puts the basket containing Jokumaraswami on Gowdathi's head. Gowdathi leaves. Music.

THE PAUNCH FELL DOWN

Basanna and Gurya meet in the street.

BASANNA. Friend Guranna, Ram Ram.

GURYA. Friend Basanna, Ram Ram.

BASANNA. Friend Guranna, why is your face downcast?

GURYA. Friend Basanna, what can I tell you? I don't know if poverty is a curse, but it certainly isn't a boon.

BASANNA. Why, my friend? I've never heard you talk with such pain. Tell me what's wrong.

GURYA. Friend, the Gowda caught me today. He somehow came to know that I had met you and he wanted to ripen my backside with his kicks.

BASANNA. If you're such a coward, who won't kick you? Has he swallowed your field?

GURYA. Where is the question of swallowing? It seems that the field is now registered in his name. Gowda has a large belly, and because he always speaks from inside that belly, what we say it can't hear, because it has no ears.

BASANNA. What a fool you are! To let a field slip away in front of your eyes. Go tell him that there are new rules and regulations.

GURYA. Debtors are always dumb.

BASANNA. Don't worry. Let me see how he takes away your field.

GURYA. You know what happened today, Basanna? Gowda set eyes on Gurupada's daughter Ningi, and didn't he get very, very hot! You know what Ningi did?

BASANNA. What did she do, my friend?

GURYA. She spat on him three times and went away.

BASANNA. That's how one should be.

GURYA. I feel very brave when Ningi is close by.

BASANNA. You want to marry her?

MELA. This is our god,
Dum Dum is his name.

Gowda and his retinue of four enter.

GOWDA. What, Gurya, you're still standing here! By the way, who's this fellow? What's his name? I seem to have seen him somewhere.

BASANNA. You want my name? Should I say it in riddles or just straight out?

ONE. He is Basanna.

GOWDA (*shuts him up and tells all four to stand in a corner*). Oh! So this is Basanna. Gurya, did you tell him what I told you?

GURYA. Sir, I haven't, but I will. Basanna, it seems your father hasn't given Gowda his share from the devil's field.

BASANNA. What field? What talk is this? Haven't you shat well this morning? Why do you blabber? There is a law by which the field belongs to the one who ploughs it. Tell him that.

GOWDA. Well, well, a great lawyer. It seems you have taken up Gurya's brief. Then you must see that he wins.

BASANNA. You don't have to tell me that.

GOWDA. Know this, all of you are living because of me.

ALL FOUR. Yes, yes, sir, yes sir.

BASANNA. Yes, yes, my lord—we all live because of your mercy, don't we?

GOWDA. Shall I show you by whose mercy you live? Gurya . . .

GURYA. Sir?

GOWDA. Bend a little. (*Gurya bends and Gowda sits on him*) By whose mercy do you live?

GURYA. My lord, by yours.

GOWDA. Tell him that.

GURYA. Basanna, I live by Gowda's mercy.

BASANNA. Ho, ho, ho, ho! Yes, yes, Gowda, in the beginning even, god used to say the same things. 'Children, you are all living because of my mercy.' But the other day, even the gods inside the temple were stolen, did you know that?

GOWDA. The thieves' arses will itch. What will they do then?

BASANNA. Impossible.

GOWDA. Impossible? Wait, I'll show you too. As from today, the field you plough is mine. Know that if you even step on that field hereafter, your legs will not be yours.

BASANNA. Gowda, shall I tell you something?

GOWDA. Tell it to his gun. I've taught it to speak. Do you hear what it says?

ALL FOUR. Dum Dum.

BASANNA. I also have a gun, but the ones I shot at don't die, they litter. (*Laughs*) Ningi was telling me that you have grey hair. Do you, Gowda?

GOWDA. Shall I show you? Here, get the gun. (*He takes the gun and Basanna puts his ear to the muzzle.*)

BASANNA. Let me hear what it says . . . I can't hear anything. (*He snatches the gun and throws it away*) Get lost, you jabbering braggart. So you'll break my legs if I step into the field. Indeed! Aren't you worried about your own legs? With aching arms, and starving bellies, my father and I cleared the forest. When men feared to pass that way even during the day, frightened of the devil's field, my father and I laboured there day and night! And now this fellow comes along and claims the field as his!

GOWDA. Gowdaship is ours for generations. Your father has written off this field to us, he has pressed his thumb at the bottom. You've come along now to change it all? Let laws and rules be made! In the end, the moneyed man is always the big man. I only have to throw six, if not three, coins and your laws and rules fall into my pocket . . . I'll give you four rupees. Will you carry my gun?

BASANNA. Well, well, you talk like a real hero. Even big kings have set up barber shops, but you haven't given up your arrogance. Shall I show you my hand? (*Sitting in front of Gurya*) Gurya, get up! Come what may, I'm behind you. Get up!

GOWDA. Doesn't a dog know whose dog it is? Doesn't it?

ALL FOUR. It does, it does.

ONE. Some curs, my lord, don't remember whose house they belong to. They hang around anyone who throws them crumbs.

BASANNA. Look, do you want to be a cur in his house? I'm like a tiger, I'm here to take care of you.

ONE. How many tigers has our Dum Dum god killed?

TWO. Eleven.

THREE. Not even a dozen?

BASANNA. Gurya, get up. Even Ningi, a young girl could stand up to Gowda and a man like you lies prone? Up!

Gurya gets up at once. Gowda falls off. The four servants stand fixed in amazement while Mela sings and Gurya begins to dance in time to the song.

MELA. The paunch fell and tumbled
On the ground.
Floating eyes, frightened eyes,
And all that mud on the whiskers!
The paunched dog sat on the back
And claimed the world as his.
He tripped and stumbled
Bang! Flat on his back.

As the song ends, the four servants lift up the Gowda. One takes Gurya's prone position and when Gowda sits on him, the others comfort him.

GOWDA. Shameless dogs. If I leave you a little free because you are poor, you climb on my head. Gurya, will you come this side?

BASANNA. Watch how the Gowda picks up courage when his dogs are around him.

GOWDA. Who is this? A fly? Here you, talk to him.

ONE. Basanna, even before the lime of your father's stone is fully dried, are you tired of living?

BASANNA. Yes, I'm so tired that I'm waiting to be killed by a brave warrior like you. Why just me? That goes for all the poor of this village.

GOWDA. I allowed this unclaimed cur to go begging in the streets and now look at its arrogance!

BASANNA. Gowda, kindly count the teeth in your mouth before you talk.

GOWDA. I stay my hand because you're young, and you challenge me? Thrash him!

The four attack Basanna. Gurya runs, screaming.

GURYA. Aiyo! Come! Gowda is killing Basanna.

GOWDA. Hey, you fellows, get back. Gurya is gathering a crowd.

The four fall back. Basanna does a push up.

BASANNA. If you're a real man, don't send your dogs, come yourself. Try your arm against mine, and know my strength. Do you think it's as easy as killing my father?

GOWDA. Why all this male talk? Shall I set you a challenge, man to man.

BASANNA. Tell me.

GOWDA (*taking out betel leaves and nuts from his pocket*). Let it be clear once and for all who's this field is, yours or mine. Let me be clear about it, you be clear, let the people be clear. Tonight is Jokumaraswami full-moon night. Whoever can sleep through tonight in the field takes the field. Are you ready? If so, take this betel.

ONE. Look, the devils are many on a full-moon night. Basanna, remember where exactly your father died before accepting the betel.

TWO. Don't you know the story of that mother of seven children?

BASANNA. I'm ready, give me the betel. (*Exits*.)

GOWDA (*calls one of the servants*). You, go to my house. Get food and a blanket. If they ask, tell them at home that Gowda will sleep in the devil's field tonight. All of you go to that field and finish the job. You can eat the food meant for me. Come and tell me later what happened. I'll be at Shari's house, understand?

ONE. Yes sir.

JOKUMARASWAMI

Gowda's house. Bassi, Shivi and Ningi are waiting for Gowdathi. Gowdathi enters with Jokumaraswami in the basket.

GOWDATHI. Bassi, how you frightened me needlessly! Shari gave it to me herself, no trouble at all! Start the worship quickly.

BASSI. Everything is ready.

Bassi, Shivi and Ningi start singing. They draw eyes and a moustache on Jokumaraswami, a snake gourd, and wrap a turban around it. Gowdathi mimes parts of the song. The rest of them dance with her.

BASSI, SHIVI. A pretty green shirt,
A dhoti of silk,
His turban at a jaunty slant—
Friend, let us worship Jokumaraswami,
Handsome Jokumaraswami!
What laughter under the moustache,
What brightness in the cheeks.
The naughty one with his brows
Ogles at the waists of flighty girls.
Isn't he Jokumaraswami?
At a hand clap he turns and glares,
Not we, but the barren ones have called you.
They await you, hands on brows—
Go kindly to them.
In their bosoms they'll hide you,

In flowers will they cover you.
Grant them fruits, great lord—
That all-high god Jokumaraswami
Do we worship.

BASSI. Now you should cook the god quickly, ma'am.

GOWDATHI. There's nothing else to be done, is there?

BASSI. No, ma'am.

GOWDATHI. Give him to me, then.

The three of them start singing again. Gowdathi cooks Jokumaraswami accordingly.

BASSI, SHIVI AND NINGI. With a golden knife, on a diamond board
How shall I cut the lord—
Into pieces long or pieces broad?
I have cut the lord.
In a golden pot, on a diamond stove
I put the lord to boil,
I boiled and cooked the dish
And of the lord I made a curry.
Come, my taster, sweet taster,
I wait with the food.
That all-high god Jokumaraswami
Do we worship.

GOWDATHI. Bassi, see if Gowda has come.

BASSI (*looks outside and comes back*). Someone seems to be coming this way. It could be Gowda.

SHIVI. I'll be going now, ma'am.

NINGI. Me too, ma'am.

GOWDATHI. Sit down, you can eat here and go later.

SHIVI. No, ma'am, the children are waiting. They'll be hungry.

Shivi and Ningi leave. 'One' of Gowda's four servants enters.

ONE. Madam . . .

GOWDATHI. Hasn't Gowda come?

ONE. No, madam.

GOWDATHI. Where has he gone?

ONE. He's gone to sleep in the field.

GOWDATHI. To the field?

ONE. That devil's field . . .

GOWDATHI. Why did he go there today of all days?

ONE. He's gone to sleep in the field to assert his ownership. He fought with Basanna, and has gone there saying, 'The field is mine—I'll sleep there.' He asked me to fetch him a blanket and some food.

GOWDATHI. Just my luck! Take the blanket.

ONE. He also asked for food.

GOWDATHI. Take the blanket and go.

She gives him a blanket. The man takes it and leaves.

BASSI. Go to bed now, ma'am. All that we've been doing since dawn has been wasted.

GOWDATHI. You go and sleep. Why should you suffer because of me?

BASSI. Then what will you do?

GOWDATHI. What else can I do? I'll fold my arms across my chest, and lie down, counting the beams on the ceiling.

BASSI. Why can't Gowda understand?

GOWDATHI (*weeping, daydreaming*). How else can I tell Gowda that I am a woman? A bird comes flying from afar and sits in its cage! It sings so that the earth itself becomes all ears and then a face, and arms and legs appear. The green breaks out and spreads. (*Sighs*) That demon behind the moon won't let go. He catches the singing bird and all that green and the flowers and shoots are no more. Once more the same barren earth, the same gaunt, leafless trees, the same empty birds' nests . . .

(*Meanwhile Bassi has left. Gowdathi sings softly*.)

Bird of distant lands, come back to your nest.
That nest swings vacant in the breeze.
Storm wind that storms,
Whirlwind that whirls,
Slip through them, my bird,
Come to me, come to me.
The watchful eyes of old Satan—
Slip past them, my bird,
Come to me, come to me.
Exhilaration hides in every branch—
Make it sprout, my bird,
Come to me, come to me.
Sing the song of that land
Till the earth is all ears
And till the green spreads again.
Come my bird, come to me,
Come to me.

She suddenly remembers something and gets up. She packs the food, takes a container of water, places it on her head and goes out. Music.

THE BIRD IS CAUGHT

A hut and a plant indicate a field. Gowda's four servants enter with the gun.

ONE. Hasn't the sheep arrived yet?

TWO. How can it? Who will come here knowingly to die?

THREE. I'm hungry, why didn't you bring food?

ONE. Gowdathi didn't give me food. She gave me the blanket, so I brought that.

FOUR. So we will have to starve here until morning.

ONE. Why until morning? Basanna will be here soon.

TWO. Do you think he'll come?

FOUR. We'll wait for about an hour or two.

THREE. If he comes after we leave?

ONE. He's not a coward, he will definitely come.

TWO. Not long ago we killed his father. And today we have to kill the son—it's a grave sin.

FOUR. Why should we bother about right and wrong?

TWO. Actually, Basanna is not at fault.

THREE. Doesn't he deny that the field was mortgaged?

TWO. You know how our Gowda has swallowed fields belonging to various people. And still you can say Basanna is wrong!

ONE. Why should we bother about all that? We'll do whatever we're asked to do. When we entered Gowda's employment, we swore before Hanuman that we would always be loyal to him, don't you remember?

TWO. That's right.

Basanna springs on them suddenly. Before anyone can do anything, he grabs the gun. They scatter, frightened.

BASANNA (*brandishing the gun*). Do you know our god's name? Dum Dum god. Here's a trigger. Behind that a bolt. You know what happens when this god says 'Dum' to people in front of him . . . they litter. You bastards, tell me where Gowda is.

ONE (*scared*). In Shari's house.

BASANNA. He sent you here to finish me off, didn't he?

ONE. Basanna . . .

BASANNA. The devil killed my father here, didn't it?

ONE. Basanna, please don't kill us, we beg you.

TWO. Basanna, please forgive us. We'll do whatever you say.

BASANNA. You'll do whatever I say?

TWO. Yes.

BASANNA. Then will you drag your arses and tell Gowda that you won't work for him any more?

ONE. Will you give us back the gun?

BASANNA. You want the gun? (*He takes aim.*)

ALL FOUR. Don't, please don't.

BASANNA. Huh! Scram then. If you show your faces just once more, I'll kill you.

All go, dragging their arses. Basanna paces about for some time, then takes the blanket left by them and goes to sleep in the hut. Gowdathi enters with food a little later.

GOWDATHI. Couldn't you have come home yourself for a minute instead of sending a servant? You fought with Basanna and came here. Couldn't you have fought tomorrow? I told you so many times to come home for dinner today. Get up, eat your food, get up! (*She serves food in the dim light of the hut. Basanna eats silently*) There's such beautiful moonlight outside, why don't you come out and eat? Gowda, how can I tell you my joy? Look at our moon, Gowda, how big he is risen. Something calls like a parrot. What's that bird? Why don't you talk? You're angry with me, aren't you, for having come out alone? Gowda, how can I tell you my agony? You are, after all, a man and you don't need children or a home. You feel you can go on like a lone owl. I am a woman. How can I live without children? Basanna has a parrot, Bassi told me. But can another's parrot be ours? I am beginning to see our parrot in front of me . . . Haven't you finished eating yet?

Basanna tugs at her sari. Gowdathi runs out happily. As the song is sung she tries to avoid him.

BASANNA. How lovely! You've come out after ages like the rising full moon.

You come, your light like a lamp of eyes lit up.
Your arms and thighs smooth like young banana stems
And lemons on your chest—
You, a bit of Paradise!
What a girl, what a complexion,
And what a slender waist,
Your eyes like mango slices
Clap hand on hand
And come sit with me.

GOWDATHI. Young man! Do you know who you are talking to? You are talking to the village's Gowdathi, a respectably married woman. Are you aware of that? Tell me where Gowda is.

BASANNA. So you want only your brave Gowda? You should've gone to whore Shari's place, he's hanging around there.

GOWDATHI. How did this blanket come to be with you?

BASANNA. He sent four dogs here to get me killed like my father. All of them got scared and left the blanket and the gun here and ran away.

GOWDATHI. Who are you, you rascal? What's your name? Your caste?

BASANNA (*laughing*). Shall I say it in prose or verse?

GOWDATHI (*stamping her foot*). Stop grinning. Give up all hopes of living and sing the song to my foot.

BASANNA. Jingling your anklets,
Thrusting out your breasts,
You want to know my name.
My name, my name,
Write it down in your breast.
The lips of all the girls
Have only my name on them,
The girls call me,
'Come, Uncle Basanna,'
The tongues of all the wives
Have only my name on them.
Their whispers say,
'Come for a moment, Basanna, our king,'
The mouths of all the hags
Have only my name on them,

They stammer, they stutter
'Come, Jokumara.'

Did you understand what I said, girl? All the girls in the village know my name, Basanna. The women know, the old, old hags know. Don't pretend you don't know me. I'm asking you from the bottom of my heart, don't say no. Come into the hut and let's talk for a while.

GOWDATHI. Who's this shameless boy—lacking
Rhythm in his mouth,
Food to eat he has not,
And yet he stands slavering before me
And wants to lick.
A chaste wife am I.
Dare you attack me?
Rinse your mouth before you speak
Or your hair I'll pull out.
Gowdas we are of this place
And my man a brave knight—
Me you'd better not pursue
Or he'll oust and kill you.

BASANNA. Ohohoho! Are you talking about your brave husband?

Are you talking about your valiant husband? Who is your husband? The one who lays every girl in the village and runs away just to show that he too is a man, is he your husband? On the day when whores' seals have to be broken, he snores under a blanket. Is he your brave man? His wife has been panting for a talking parrot for ten years and he couldn't get it—is he your husband?

What kind of a life is that? You're suffering under an illusion.

Don't refuse, laughing. My life you hold,
And fondle in your palm,
Don't make excuses
For refusing my friendship.

GOWDATHI. Basanna, why commit this sin knowingly? Listen to what I tell you.

BASANNA. Go ahead, girl, tell me prettily.

GOWDATHI. I am another's wife.
Don't pursue me, Basanna.
Remember what happened to Ravana?
You laugh, you come running,
You ogle, with hands outstretched.
Know, you imbecile, proper behaviour.
I am a married woman.
You dare not risk my enmity,
Know, you rascal, of right and wrong.

BASANNA. There's no right or wrong after eating Jokumaraswami curry.
Don't tell me.
Don't show me the bundle of scriptures.
I've read many books and
All of them say
That a man and woman should unite.

Girl, did you understand what I have been saying? Where is the question of right and wrong after eating Jokumaraswami curry? You came and fed me Jokumaraswami, do you think I'll let you go now? Only after I ate what you fed me did I start wanting you. You ignore the one who has a talking parrot and search for it elsewhere. How do you expect to find it? Come, be friends with me, ask me for whatever bird you want.

Why don't you see, you hot, well-fed wench?
I implore, I'm at your feet,
Come to me, come to me.
I shall give you a bird that flies,
A lovely parrot that talks,
I shall adorn your hair with flowers, girl,
I implore, I'm at your feet,
Come to me, come to me.
Look at the full moon,
Listen to the birds sing,
Stop resisting!
The eastern wind sweeps, girl.
I implore, I'm at your feet,
Come to me, come to me.

Do you understand, girl? For ten years you've yearned for a bird, when the bird flies onto your lap you say you don't want it. How can you do that?

GOWDATHI. What shall I do? A singing parrot on one side, a husband with daggers in his eyes on the other. Basanna, why do you want to die needlessly? Just make way for me.

BASANNA. All this happened only after I ate what was put before me. Go if you want to, I won't stop you. I'm not the kind to lay an unwilling woman. As you go, drop by Shari's house on the way—you can pick up Gowda there.

GOWDATHI. He said he would be going to the field to sleep and yet he has gone there.

BASANNA. Here's another bit of news: Gowda now wants Gurupada's daughter Ningi.

GOWDATHI. What!

BASANNA. Ask Shari.

A parrot screeches.

GOWDATHI. Isn't that a bird screeching in the hut?

BASANNA. Oh that? My talking parrot. Who knows, the cage might have fallen down, or maybe it saw a snake.

GOWDATHI. Quickly go and see what has happened.

BASANNA. What's the use of having the parrot if you don't want it?

GOWDATHI. When did I say I didn't want it?

BASANNA. Come, then.

Basanna gets the cage from inside the hut. Gowdathi is excited at seeing it.

GOWDATHI. Nothing's wrong I hope?

BASANNA. No.

GOWDATHI. Does it talk?

BASANNA. You haven't heard it speak yet. All the girls in the village are amazed at hearing it talk. It tells such wonderful stories.

GOWDATHI. I want to hear this parrot talk and tell stories. Basanna, Basanna . . .
Inside the hut,
My beloved,
Let's go

Let's talk to the bird.
The eastern wind sweeps,
The flowers and trees bloom,
The bird's song is heard—
Let's talk to the bird.

THE DEFEAT OF DUM DUM GOD

MELA. The Gowda wanders about
Day and night
And calls it 'love'—
Chasing a chick,
Chasing Ningi.
Three months he's been wandering
Like a cockerel
Crowing each dawn,
Deserting his field, his home,
Shameless.
But the chick has flown into Gurya's basket.

As the song is being sung, we see Gowda grabbing at Ningi, running behind her as she escapes, and so on.

GOWDA. You have been eluding me for three months. The day I saw you, I bought some spice, and now I have caught you, my bird! Now don't be difficult, let's go.

NINGI. Shameless fellow, take your spice, sprinkle it on your wife and lick it. If you talk like this again, I'll put the same spice on you.

GOWDA. That's exactly what I'm saying. You put it on me, I'll put it on you. Today you'll either be mine or you'll go to the tomb of the dead.

NINGI. Really, my god! He is so brave! Brave man, twirl your moustaches, are they blunt?

GOWDA. I have left them like that so that you can play with them after I have you in the palm of my hand.

NINGI. My god! So brave! Brave man, Basanna has come, run away quick!

GOWDA. Crazy girl. How naughty you are. You know that I always get what I want. Why do you give me the run around? I've left the house, the field, the earth, to wander shamelessly after you. All the girls in the village are crazy about that Basanna. What will you get by chasing him? That starving bastard labours in my field. What can he give you? Ask me for whatever you want, wear and eat whatever you want, take these thousand rupees if you want. Jingle, jingle, jingle . . . can you hear?

NINGI. I can.

GOWDA. Then come with me.

NINGI. What will my parents say?

GOWDA. They are so poor, what can they say to a Gowda? Come with me and I'll build you a two-storeyed house. I'll get a swinging bed made for you and give you a slave to swing it, or else I'll place you in a glass case. I'll also get you a husband, if you want.

NINGI. Husband? If you keep me, who will be willing to marry me?

GOWDA. Why do you worry? You know our Gurya. I'll get him to marry you. The name is the husband's but the game is mine!

NINGI. Is that so? Gurya is here, shall I call him? Gurya . . .

Gurya enters. Gowda is scared at the sight of him.

GURYA. Hello, Gowda sir. I'll marry this lady now that you've said so.

GOWDA. Come here, you bastard!

GURYA. Bastard? I thought I was born to my father. Or are you my father?

GOWDA. Why, you whore's son!

GURYA. Didn't I say you were my father? Why did you call me, Father?

GOWDA. You! You let your tongue run loose before this whore?

GURYA. She's not a whore. I'm her husband. Or rather, we aren't married yet, but the engagement has been held.

GOWDA. You and Ningi, getting married? Why, are all the men of the village dead?

Ningi giggles.

GURYA. Why, am I not a man?

GOWDA. You loafer, shut up.

GURYA. Arrey! It's not a lie. Wait! Wife, come here! Gowda is not convinced of our marriage. Fall at my feet. (*Ningi falls at Gurya's feet*) May you have a house full of children and die laughing.

GOWDA. You eat my food and now you have the audacity to talk against me! Ingrate!

GURYA. This woman is very bad, sir. If you are with her, you feel very brave. That's why I'll marry her. (*Both laugh.*)

GOWDA. Don't laugh, I'll tear you apart.

GURYA. We don't talk when we have something to say. We just laugh. We can convey anything by laughing. Shall I show you? (*Laughs questioningly*) Do you know what I just said? Wife, how does Gowda's gun talk? (*Ningi giggles*) What Ningi means is that it goes 'poof!'

GOWDA. You bastard, are you sick of life?

GURYA. I was. I went to the field thinking, 'If I can marry Ningi, I won't be.' She had also come to the field. Look at my luck. You went around with your gun, gold and silver, and crowed like a cockerel for three months, but the lady didn't even look at you. I, too, crowed like a cockerel and the chick came to me. The moment I clutched and caressed it, it was mine. That's why I'm getting married. Don't think this is said in jest. Ask Basanna if you want. He was a witness.

GOWDA. I know all about this whore and Basanna.

GURYA. Really? Basanna has been sleeping in your field for three months now, do you know that?

GOWDA. You son of a bitch!

He tries to kick him; Gurya pulls his leg and Gowda falls down.

GURYA. Who is the son of a bitch, you or me?

NINGI. Husband, you shouldn't talk to the Gowda like that.

GURYA. That's right! Gowda, Basanna had a parrot and he gave it to Gowdathi. Gowdathi swallowed it, and now her tummy is like this! Isn't it so, Wife?

NINGI. It's obvious if you see her.

GOWDA. You bastard! If this news is true, you are safe. If not, there won't be eyes in your face even if you want to shed tears. Wait and see! (*Exits.*)

GURYA. Wait, we still have to clap our hands and laugh.

They both clap and dance to music.

THE GOD IS SLAIN

Basanna is sitting in the field near the hut. Gowdathi comes running.

BASANNA. Come, come my love! I've been waiting for a long time . . .

GOWDATHI. Basanna . . .

BASANNA. What?

GOWDATHI. Gowda knows all about us.

BASANNA. So what? Why should you worry? You can stay at my house.

GOWDATHI. Will Gowda leave you alone?

BASANNA. Silly, do you think I'll die if a street dog barks, or a fly flaps its wings? Let him get to know. I know your husband's bravery well. One grunt and he'll drop his gun and run.

GOWDATHI. Do you know what I dreamt yesterday?

BASANNA. What?

GOWDATHI. There was a forest in the dream, and in the forest a cave. As your hard chest caressed my tender breasts, as lightning split the cloud, as wind filled the bamboo, I felt you calling me from inside the cave. Then came the sound of whistling, like an old owl. When I got up, I saw Gowda pacing about outside, whistling. Basanna, this will be our last meeting.

BASANNA. You get scared very easily.

GOWDATHI. You've always listened to me patiently. Why don't you believe me today? Every night you've shone and shone, merging with this clay you shone. How can I bear to see you die in front of my eyes? All of them have plotted to kill you. Gowda will come today with five hundred rogues to slay you. Go, escape quickly.

BASANNA. Aiyaya! Five hundred rogues? Let them come. None of them have sucked their mother's milk, and I haven't grown up on dog's milk. I'll smear their faces with mud and send them scooting before you can say 'Ha'!

GOWDATHI. Aiyo! All the husbands of the wives you have laid, and the men of the women, will come together. Please listen to me.

BASANNA. Let them come, let them come. All their women have tasted my body. Let their fellows taste my fist.

GOWDATHI. Basanna, I saw the light of a torch, come, get up.

BASANNA. Oh that? They're only fireflies. They come every day to light the tamarind tree.

GOWDATHI. Aiyo! How can I make you believe me? Basanna, this is no time to argue.

BASANNA. I'm staying here even if they come. You can go if you are scared.

GOWDATHI. Oh! Basanna! What shall I do!

What shall I do!
The Gowda comes to slay you!
Scoundrels and rascals with sticks
Are raring to get at you,
What shall I do!
The Gowda comes to slay you!
There is no refuge
Even in the forest. There is no one to put some
Sense into those useless bums!
What shall I do!
The Gowda comes to slay you!

(A scream is heard from afar.)

Basanna, open your eyes and see! They're not fireflies! They are murderers. There are five hundred against one. What can you do alone?

BASANNA. You're right. Look, no torches can be seen in this direction. Run.

GOWDATHI. How can I leave you alone and go?

BASANNA. I'll definitely join the talking parrot wherever it is. Run away.

GOWDATHI. If we have to run, we'll go together. Or else let me die with you.

BASANNA. The parrot's life is more precious than our lives. Run and save the parrot's life, don't stand here arguing uselessly. You will find me wherever the parrot is.

GOWDATHI. You ask me to run?

BASANNA. Quickly.

GOWDATHI. You?

BASANNA. There you go again!

GOWDATHI. Shall I run?

BASANNA. Run, quickly. (*Gowdathi runs. Basanna stands looking after her*) The crazy girl has forgotten about me in her tummy. (*He looks around and takes up a sickle hanging on a tree. Before he can attack them bravely, he is surrounded by people wielding sickles and torches. Gowda is seen with his gun. Although alarmed, Basanna speaks up courageously*) What, Gowda, come to see the field?

Even as he is saying this, a man hits him from behind at Gowda's signal. Basanna falls. They pick him up a like a log and scream and dance.

ALL. Slay, slay the village rascal! Son of a whore, Basanna, get up! Gowdathi is calling.
Luring girls
With a talking parrot,
Claiming all the fields as his—

Let's make mincemeat out of him
With one blow.
Let's feed him to the eagle,
Let him mingle with the slush.

As the song ends, Gowda throws Basanna onto the ground and shoots him. The stage hushes as Basanna screams 'Aaah'. After some time, Sutradhara's voice is heard in the silence.

SUTRADHARA. Count, and they are five hundred.
Coun, and the hands are a thousand
Which grip and chop the tender god.
A thousand hands, in each hand
A sickle or an axe,
Which slash to death the tender god.
Killed and thrown him,
They have slashed and thrown him,
And the flowing blood
Fills the river and the pond.
Where the blood falls,
Springs the sprout and the shoot,
And all the earth is fresh, is green.
Let a good government rule us,
Let children play in all homes,
May he who sows own the field,
May the country be filled with wealth and grain.
Come, my little lord,
Come, my pretty moon,
Come, Jokumaraswami!

Curtain.

SAMBA SHIVA

A Farce

Translated from the Kannada by
Padma Ramachandra Sharma

A NOTE ON THE TRANSLATION

As is inevitable, perhaps, in any translation, some of the colour of the original words with bawdy connotations might have been diluted. Groups interested in staging this play should fill in exclamations, insults and epithets in their own kind of English, preferably with sexual connotations. (For example, one of the words translated here as 'bastard' literally means in Kannada, 'son of a shaven widow', which is obviously more colourful, but would require explanation for non-Indian audiences.) The language of the King, in particular, slips constantly between high sounding and vulgar.

Stage directions are not given in the way usual in English-language plays, but basics of the set design and movements, where not given, can easily be deduced from the text.

Lines written as verse are intended to be sung.

Padma Ramachandra Sharma
1991

DIRECTOR'S NOTE

Six years ago, in 1985, when I decided to produce the play *Samba Shiva: A Farce*, I hadn't even read it! I had just heard the storyline from Dr Kambar. I knew something about the theatre style in which it was being written. We managed to get the manuscript only a few days before rehearsals began. After reading it, I realized that I had not made a mistake in choosing this play. There is something about it which struck me as unique; and it has turned out to be one of our repertory's most successful productions.

Till then I had not produced any play by Kambar, except the children's play *Alibaba*. I had read, seen and been impressed by all his major plays from *Rishyashringa* to *Jokumaraswami*; but I did not dare to produce any of them. This was probably because of their pronounced folk character, which made them very interesting to read or see. But the thought of staging them always evoked a fear in my mind—a feeling that these plays would turn out as imitations of stock theatre forms. The theatre scene at the time was partially responsible for this feeling.

In the 60s, the new wave which sought to correlate the folk and the modern had already begun, and Kambar was a major figure in this movement. His *Jokumaraswami* had electrified the theatre with its folk structure. The feudal master, the servant who is the strong male, the women who turn between the two (symbolic of earth), the sinewy language and the songs in the play—all these had made a vivid impact on Kannada culture. They had even entered the company dramas and popular cinema. This is probably why almost all the productions of *Jokumaraswami* struck me as meaningless repetitions.

But reading *Samba Shiva* was a novel experience. Though there are many things in it which are characteristic of Kambar, it is a break from his earlier plays. He has given up the invariable metaphor of the 'woman and earth' along with the stock characters and plots which revolve round this theme. Secondly, he has not used the language of South Karnataka but the common language of the lower classes of Bangalore. Thirdly, the solemnity of folk ritual seen in his other plays is absent here. This play is rich with the chafing wit of street drama.

This newness is probably the result of a change in his attitude towards folk and traditional structures. The earlier plays were inspired by bayalata, open-air performances and other folk forms. But this play draws from company drama, popular cinema and even Western comedy.

Samba Shiva is not only a major play but also an important landmark in the theatre movement. The playwrights of the 60s who had modelled their work on Kambar's had begun to realize by 1980 that their approach failed to express the modern sensibility. They were in search of new models which would correlate the traditional with the modern. A new phase had begun in the theatre movement. With *Samba Shiva,* Kambar initiated this phase. *Jokumaraswami* is based on the bayalata form. Kambar himself called it 'modern bayalata', indicating both the possibilities and the limitations of the play. The playwright strains to impose the bayalata structure on what is essentially a modern experience. A close study shows that he has even tried to simplify this modern experience to fit the bayalata structure. The archetypal characters of *Jokumaraswami*, the archetypal revolution which takes place, the slogan 'The tiller is the owner of the land' which comes through as a folk moral—all these are examples of such a simplification.

But *Samba Shiva* does not have a pre-ordained form like *Jokumaraswami*. We can only trace a few inspirations: bayalata, company drama, popular cinema and post-realistic Western drama. So *Samba Shiva* is neither modern bayalata nor modern company drama. It is a modern play. Another interesting aspect of this play is that it is a comedy. This is Kambar's first pure comedy. It is also a new experiment in this form. Contemporary playwrights writing comedies model their work mostly on Western plays. Pure comedy is rare in Kannada theatre. But *Samba Shiva* tries to explore this form by going back to our roots.

Actually, the newness in *Samba Shiva* is related to the fact that it is a comedy. Like *Jokumaraswami*, *Samba Shiva* too tells the story of the overthrow of a lecherous king. But here even the rebels are seen through the eyes of a comic writer. This gives it a liveliness and playful quality, an attitude towards the folk and the traditional which is quite new.

These new perspectives in *Samba Shiva* became crucial to my production of the play. The play does not imitate any particular folk form. It does not borrow any traditional rhythm, dance, music, language or costume. The folk qualities here are integral to the structure of the play. I tried to find a design that would take all this into account. The play also led me to incorporate some elements of popular cinema and company drama into the folk mould.

I am indebted to *Samba Shiva* for bringing about a new attitude towards 'folkism'. It has shown us a fresh way of encountering our theatre tradition without finding refuge in folk forms.

K. V. Akshara

Samba Shiva: A Farce was first produced in the original Kannada by Ninasam at Heggodu on 30 September 1985. It was also produced throughout Karnataka under the banner of 'Ninasam Tirugat' during the year 1985–86, with the following cast:

SAMBA	Nataraj Enagi
SHIVA	K. S. Ramesh
GANESH, MESSENGER AND POLICE	Krishna Kumar
DING DONG AND WHITE ELEPHANT	Sarat K. S.
KING	Channabasappa
CHAMBERLAIN	Ashok A. V.
RICHMAN, SMALL CHANGE, WASHERMAN AND BIRAYYA	H. S. Prasanna
MINISTER	K. G. Krishna Murthy
GAJANIMBE	Sushila
GODAVARI	Usha Halkere
CHORUS	Prabhakar, Nagaraj K. N. and Vidya Hegade
DIRECTION	K. V. Akshara
MUSIC	Chandrasekhar Kambar

It was also produced and directed by Ekbal Ahemed for Natya Sangha Theatre Centre, Bangalore, on 30 March 1990.

PROLOGUE

DIRECTOR.

Greetings!
Today we are putting on for you a major comedy,
that is, a farce.
As you would give measurements to a tailor
to get a shirt stitched, so
we gave the poet the measurements of our minds and yours and he wrote this play specially for us. All the spices you need for your entertainment are in this play—
there is love, sex and revolution,
politics,
there are dialogues, songs and dances and a circus, and there is also a cabaret.
There are men and women who are not a mixture of both, and that third kind is there too.
It may be shocking to the bourgeois,
but the stealthy pleasures that bring happiness within are also there.
If you catch a cold with surprise, never mind.
I will tell you one secret straight away—
the hero of this play is a donkey!
Donkey becomes Minister and King becomes Donkey,
the disinherited hold their revolution
and the revolutionaries become pimps,
male becomes female, there's a marriage

of a she-ass, etc.
But—
these days we have forgotten how to laugh.
Laughter has become the great task
of the generosity of common people.
Please remember how you used to laugh
and how your ancestors used to laugh
and do us the favour
of laughing like that.
We have collected jokes from
various sources to make you laugh.
This is the kind of play where looking at each other—
and that means
us looking at you—
and you looking at us—
we must all laugh.

SCENE ONE

The Ganesha temple on the outskirts of the city. The god is missing from the altar. Present are Samba and Shiva, father and son. It is obvious that they have been fighting. Samba slowly takes out a bottle of toddy.

SHIVA. Women and drink—if you have them, nothing else matters to you. This is a temple. Don't drink here at least.

SAMBA. The great god himself gets thirsty. Why shouldn't human beings? God knows all about it. And you think you're god's pet and can speak on his behalf! It's you who have given me the title of drunken rake. Shouldn't I at least live up to it, son?

SHIVA. Don't call me son. I get angry. *You* can call yourself my father but I won't. No father wants to get married before his son does.

SAMBA. I can say the same thing. Call yourself a son? 'My poor, lonely father shivering in the cold. He needs a companion.' Have you ever said anything like that since your mother died? You open your mouth only to say that you want to get married. You're not old enough either. At your age, I was not even wearing knickers. (*Drinks.*)

SHIVA. I'll come right to the point, Father. I won't stand for you coming in the way of my marriage.

SAMBA. When have I ever done that?

SHIVA. Who broke up the alliance from Chikanalli? Wasn't it you?

SAMBA. Why would I do that? Shouldn't a father feel happy when his son marries? Won't your wife be my daughter-in-law?

SHIVA. Then why did those people say no in the end?

SAMBA. They must have looked at your mug.

SHIVA. I know what you told them in secret.

SAMBA. In secret? Whatever was that?

SHIVA. Didn't you say that your son wasn't interested in marrying so young? Didn't you offer yourself instead?

SAMBA. I did say that, but only after they said no to you. Your mother knew what an honest soul I was. Do you know what she would have said if she had been alive today? 'Son, your father is telling the truth. Believe him.' That's what she would have said.

SHIVA. Mother was the one you lied to most. Quite a few of your exploits came to light even while she was alive.

SAMBA. Just five or six. That wasn't much at my age.

SHIVA. Mother died of your lies.

SAMBA. You'll be the same after marriage. Can a wife ever be told the truth? You should only pretend to tell the truth, but in truth it should all be lies. Remember.

SHIVA. You should remember too. You don't come trailing behind me for my sake. I know that. You are looking at brides for me but your real intention is to carry them off yourself. A fine father you are!

SAMBA. That's all very well, but why can't you at least be big-hearted and say that you'll marry after I do?

SHIVA. At least you've been married once.

SAMBA. But she is dead. Would I have asked you otherwise?

SHIVA. I haven't been married even once.

SAMBA. Later you can marry four times. I'm in a hurry right now. Get me married! I saw your mother in my dreams last night.

SHIVA. Pure lies.

SAMBA. No. It's the real truth. 'Listen, you must marry again. Promise!' That's what she said in my dream.

SHIVA. Bravo! (*Laughs*.)

SAMBA. You're laughing, aren't you? You rascal, do you know how much your mother and I loved each other?

SHIVA. You started fighting as soon as you looked at each other in the morning.

SAMBA. We'd still be fighting if she was alive. But in my dream we didn't fight. I gave her my word of honour that I'd marry again. Only then did she leave me. Otherwise, she stubbornly refused to leave. Do you understand?

SHIVA. She was in my dream too, last night. She said, 'Don't let your father marry.' Not just that. She told me not to believe a word of what you said.

SAMBA. You bloody liar. How can she appear in two dreams at the same time?

SHIVA. That only proves that she was not in your dream.

SAMBA. You son of a bitch. You're no son of mine.

SHIVA. You lecher! You are no father of mine.

SAMBA. If I am a lecher, what would your mother be?

SHIVA. If I am a son of a bitch, what would your wife be?

SAMBA. Ugh!

SHIVA. Ugh!

(*They sit quietly for some time*.)

Father.

SAMBA. Don't talk. I warn you.

SHIVA. It's cold outside. Drink a little more.

SAMBA. That's my son. If only you'd also say I could marry again . . .

SHIVA. Let's think of something. What about getting married on the same day?

SAMBA. To the same girl?

SHIVA. No, different ones.

SAMBA. That's more like it.

SHIVA. Anyway, I've seen a girl. You must help me now. If you have anyone in mind, I will help you. Mutual cooperative society. What do you say?

SAMBA. Fine. Tell me what I must do now.

SHIVA. You must wear a sari.

SAMBA. What!

SHIVA. Didn't I tell you they need a maid in her house?

SAMBA. Yes . . .

SHIVA. That's it. If you want to help your son, dress up in a sari and start working there. I will come there to see you. It will give me an excuse. Later on, if there is someone you fancy, I'll help you out.

SAMBA. Bravo, son! What if I don't agree?

SHIVA. I will die.

SAMBA. I think you'd better die.

SHIVA. Really! Of all people, I had to go and talk to you about my troubles. Please shut up now.

SAMBA. All right, then. I won't speak again. If I could, I would say something: 'You idiot, I was born before you. It's better for me to marry first.

If I marry, you'll have a mother. You'll have proper meals at proper times. Your wife will have a mother-in-law who can scold her'. . . etc.

SHIVA. Ugh, is it so difficult to shut up? (*Biting his lips*) I get . . . I get very angry.

SAMBA. Don't show me your teeth like that. I'm not a dentist. What I was telling you was that I won't talk to you any more. That's all. If I did, I wanted to tell you:

How can I get a wife, oh how?
How can I bear being parched and burnt?
I fret and I don't know the way.
How will I get a wife?

Hey, Shiva, we must sing a song like that on the white notes. Then this play will start sparkling.

SHIVA. All right. That means I am an orphan, I have had neither food nor drink for two days. Nobody cares. I'm not breathing, just sighing. Nobody cares. I toss and turn and can't sleep. Nobody cares. Why should I go on living? I'll go inside and hang myself. Then you can live in peace.

SAMBA. All right.

SHIVA. Even if you call, I won't open the door.

SAMBA. Of course not! You'll have hanged yourself. How can you open the door?

SHIVA. You'll feel sorry later.

SAMBA. I feel sorry even now.

SHIVA. Oh no! There isn't even a god in this wretched temple who can listen to my woes. (*Goes into the sanctuary and shuts the door.*)

SAMBA. What a son! Kill himself, indeed! Let me see how he manages it. Anyway, we came here to the capital looking for girls. No friends, no acquaintances. Just when were thinking of going back, this fellow sees a girl. In some alley. There's a house in the alley, and a beauty on the balcony, combing her hair. He stands there, with his mouth open. She smiles, the crafty girl. Shouldn't he ask himself who she's smiling at? He smiles too. I also smile, but that's a different story. From that moment the fever sets in. Sighing all day, dreaming, talking to himself, singing . . . the lot! I want to use my son as a pretext to snap up a girl, but I'm not succeeding, damn it! He's my only son.

We've got to depend on each other. That's the only way I can find consolation, but he wants to get married first. Fine! Let it be that way. It was much nicer in the past. Bhishma wouldn't marry when his father asked him to. 'No, Father, it is you who should marry'—that's what he said. We don't have children like that any more. (*He lies down.*)

Ganesha enters. A donkey comes with him.

GANESHA. No devotees, no worship. I can't even go back to my mother and father and relax. This wretched donkey. It follows me wherever I go. It starts braying if I am out of sight for a minute. Who would be generous enough to take it, even if I were to give it away? Only Shiva, my father, can save me. (*Looking at the closed door*) Oh, someone's here too. (*Knocking*) Who's there? Open the door!

Samba gets up and sees Ganesha.

SAMBA. Greetings!

GANESHA. Who is inside?

SAMBA. Sir, your makeup is very impressive.

GANESHA. What makeup? Who on earth are you?

SAMBA. Speak to me with respect. I'm not a nice fellow. If I get angry . . .

GANESHA (*to himself*). This is strange. People fall at my feet when they see me and ask for boons. This fellow has the guts to shout at me. All right (*Addressing Samba*), my good man . . .

SAMBA. No, no, there's no need for such courtesy.

GANESHA. Don't be so bashful, I just called you a good man.

SAMBA. My name is Samba. Call me that.

GANESHA. I see. Well, Samba, who is inside?

SAMBA. My son, Shiva. He's quite healthy except that he's been struck by the disease you call love in your plays. He couldn't get the girl, so he's gone inside to hang himself.

GANESHA. Ugh! Was this the only place he could find to die? Call him out.

SAMBA. I will. Take off your makeup.

GANESHA. Look. I'm not a dressed-up Ganesha. I'm real. This is my temple. I was fed up with sitting on the pedestal. So I just went for a little walk. That's all. Now make him open the door.

SAMBA (*to himself*). Oh, I see. He doesn't belong to a drama troupe as I thought at first. More likely an inmate of a lunatic asylum. (*Loudly*) Sir, are you not Ganesha, the son of Parvati? I shall pray to you. Will you grant me a boon?

GANESHA. There is no need to sing and pray.

SAMBA. Oh, no. Traditions can't be dropped like that. After all, if anything is wasted, it'll only be a song. Here you are:

> Lord Ganesha, son of Parvati,
> we bow and salute you!
> Son of Shiva, destroyer of obstacles,
> we fold our hands to you!

Wherever we stand or fall, stretch out
your hands to protect us.
Give us wisdom, enough to know
the difference between lime and butter,
enough to know the difference between
the donkey's tail and its head!

Right. That's over. Sir, grant me a boon now.

GANESHA. I have nothing to give you. I am a pauper. What can a god living in an abandoned temple give?

SAMBA. You kept quiet while I was singing and now you say you have nothing. Show me some magic at least.

GANESHA. What? Magic?

SAMBA (*to himself*). Didn't my son want me to become a woman? (*Loudly*) Yes, make me a woman.

GANESHA. What? A woman?

SAMBA. Yes. Aren't you a god? Let us see if you can do it.

GANESHA. You want to be a woman permanently or temporarily?

SAMBA. I just want to see what you can do. Come on . . .

GANESHA. All right, then. You see this pearl? Put it in your mouth. (*He gives it to him. Samba is about to put it in his mouth*) No, not here. There, where you're hidden. Go and put it in your mouth. (*Samba goes to where Ganesha indicates, immediately turns into a woman and comes running back.*)

SAMBA. Oh, my god. I'm sorry. I didn't realize you were the real Ganesha. I fall at your feet, Father. Make me a man again. Please. I shall really pray now.

Ganesha, protect me, Father!
I can't bear to look like this.
If you can, make me a man now, Father!

GANESHA. Take the pearl out of your mouth.

Samba does so happily and gives the pearl back.

SAMBA. Thanks, god!

GANESHA. Now will you get the door opened?

SAMBA. Oh, I was forgetting. (*Knocking on the door*) Shiva, open the door! Lord Ganesha himself is here. Open the door!

SHIVA. Who? God? I don't know him.

SAMBA. Really, he is a real god.

SHIVA. Let him grant a boon if he is a god.

SAMBA. Well then, open the door and ask for something.

SHIVA. No, I won't. I'll open the door only after he grants me a boon.

GANESHA. A sticky customer! Hey, you! Who are you anyway? Will you come out or shall I call the police?

SAMBA. Great god! Why do you get angry with a poor devotee? If you will only toss him a boon . . .

GANESHA. Honestly, I don't have anything. Shall I just bless him?

SAMBA. Hey, Shiva! He will bless you. Open the door.

SHIVA. Anyone can give an empty-handed blessing. I shall open the door only when he grants me a boon.

GANESHA. What a predicament! All I have with me is a donkey. Would you like it?

SHIVA. What would I do with it? Wait on it?

GANESHA. Don't imagine it's an ordinary donkey. It's called Ding Dong. Do you know how it came into being? There was an artist. He used to stay in this very temple. I used to be bored stiff, sitting on the pedestal all the time. So I made friends with him. He used to brag that he could paint a person just by looking at his hair. So I thought I would test his artistry. Once I found a strand of hair belonging to the King of this city. I brought it to the artist and asked him to paint a picture. He did, and it was the picture of a donkey. We burst out laughing. As I laughed, I brought the picture to life. That is the donkey over there.

SAMBA. Not bad at all.

GANESHA. It'll do as you say. You could build up a circus company with it. And that's not all. This donkey is destined to become king.

SAMBA. Shiva, he's giving you the donkey. Open the door!

Shiva opens the door, sees Ganesha and rushes to fall at his feet with great devotion. Ganesha escapes equally quickly, runs in and shuts the door.

GANESHA. Look here! The only thing I have is this donkey. That is the boon I have granted you. Take it and go away.

SHIVA. You're some god! You said you'd bless me.

GANESHA (*opening the door*). I have done that too. Now get lost, both of you!

SHIVA. What was your blessing?

GANESHA. What do you want?

SHIVA. Only that I should get the girl I desire.

GANESHA. The donkey will help you get the girl too. Go away.

SAMBA. Sir! Can I have the pearl? You won't need it because you are celibate.

GANESHA. I told you, it's not mine.

SAMBA. Just for a day or two. Then I'll give it back. Please, lord!

GANESHA. You won't go back on your word, will you?

SAMBA. Impossible! Can a god be deceived?

GANESHA. You people deceive god more than anyone else. Anyway, take the pearl, but give it back when I ask for it (*As he closes the door, Ganesha hands over the pearl.*)

SAMBA. Just a minute! Bless us again so that our donkey play may be enacted smoothly.

GANESHA. So be it!

SCENE TWO

Palace. King and Policeman.

KING. How is the police security?

POLICEMAN. It is satisfactory, my lord!

KING. Any rebellion, revolution, etc.?

POLICEMAN. Nothing at all, my lord. They have all been thrown into jail.

KING. Send in the Chamberlain. I want to speak to him in private. You stand outside.

POLICEMAN. As you command, my lord. (*He goes out.*)

Chamberlain comes in.

KING. Hey, Chamberlain! Did you find her?

CHAMBERLAIN. I am trying my best, my lord.

KING. For how long? Won't I be ridiculed if people come to know that the great King of Shivapura cannot get a lovely girl he fancies? Did you search every house in town?

CHAMBERLAIN. I did, my lord.

KING. Didn't you find any women?

CHAMBERLAIN. There are women. But the one wearing a green sari and a blue blouse cannot be traced. But I assure you I'll find her very soon. I have learnt something recently. It seems she is the merchant's daughter.

KING. Green sari, blue blouse—remember, son! Don't you forget. Oh, what a beauty! A garden—Chamberlain, just imagine—a garden . . .

POLICEMAN (*comes in and salutes*). A delegation of important citizens to see you, my lord.

KING. Didn't you tell them that we were having a private conversation?

POLICEMAN. I did, my lord. But they insist on seeing you.

KING. Why?

POLICEMAN. The petition is here, my lord.

KING. Just read the summary in one sentence.

POLICEMAN (*reading*). Alas, our lives are cursed! Tax if you sit, tax if you stand, tax if you brush your teeth, tax if you put on your clothes, A tax, B tax, C tax . . . The summary is that the people are suffering under the weight of their taxes.

KING. I understand. Why are you still standing here? Don't you dare come in again until our private conversation is finished. You'll be flayed alive! (*The Policeman rushes out, frightened*) Damn these people! They spoil the mood. What was I saying?

CHAMBERLAIN. A beautiful garden . . .

KING. Yes, that's right. A garden, Chamberlain, a lovely garden. Birds and shrubs chirping! Somewhere a nightingale kicking up dust. Moonlight pouring forth like rice flour! Then that beauty, that girl in a green sari and a blue blouse will make her entrance, singing happily, dancing gaily, the bells on her anklets jingling, accompanied by pipes and drums! Has she come?

CHAMBERLAIN. Yes, my lord, she has come. By the way, am I also allowed in the garden, my lord?

KING. Yes, of course. How can I love without your cooperation? But come quietly so that the grazing nightingale doesn't run away.

CHAMBERLAIN. A nightingale grazing? Isn't it a bird, my lord?

KING. It's an animal. If you say it's a bird, I'll break your teeth.

CHAMBERLAIN. Yes, yes, it must be an animal. It must have four legs.

KING. A long tail, a face like a horse, but small ears. It looks up at the sky, stiffens its tail and brays. We have many of them in our garden. That is our national animal, my son.

CHAMBERLAIN. Yes, yes! At first, listening to you speak, I was reminded of a donkey.

KING. There is a story about that. A donkey is like a man. It brays when bored. But I still don't feel enthusiastic towards it because it kicks. Only kings should have the right to kick. What do you say?

CHAMBERLAIN. Of course.

KING. These damned revolutionaries want the right to kick, too!

CHAMBERLAIN. Isn't that wrong?

KING. Oh, look! You've forgotten the garden. You've left her standing there. What happens next?

CHAMBERLAIN. Well, it's like this, my lord. Let's imagine the girl is there. You are here. I am by her side.

KING. Why should you be by her side? I'll be near her. You be here.

CHAMBERLAIN. No, no, just imagine, that's all.

KING. All right, but let's imagine the way I want to.

CHAMBERLAIN. I've just brought her, my lord. That's why she's beside me. Now she will come towards you.

KING. I see. That's all right then.

CHAMBERLAIN. You are here and she has come. How will you be standing? Please show me.

KING. Like this?

CHAMBERLAIN. It would be better to be more stylish.

KING. Now?

CHAMBERLAIN. That's better. Imagine I'm her. I have come. What will you do now?

KING. What shall I do?

CHAMBERLAIN. Bend over and purr.

KING (*bending over*). Purr, purr, purr.

CHAMBERLAIN. Not like that, my lord. As she comes near you, smile at her, say 'beloved' and throw a kiss at her. (*Demonstrates*) Let's see you do it now.

KING. Beloved . . .

CHAMBERLAIN. No, not like that. You should throw your kiss with such style that she will throw her heart at you in the same style. That's how stylish you should be.

KING. Your face looked like a used napkin. Should I look like that too?

CHAMBERLAIN. You do it your own way.

KING. Beloved!

CHAMBERLAIN. Now, you kneel down, hold your hands over your heart and speak. Shall I pretend to be the girl again? (*He comes over coquettishly*.)

KING. Oh dear! I feel very shy.

CHAMBERLAIN. She should be the one to feel shy. Don't you think so, my lord?

KING. Then you show me what to do and what to say.

CHAMBERLAIN. Imagine you are the girl. I'm you and I'm kneeling here like this. (*Kneels, hands on chest*) Beloved, I must tell you something straightaway. My soul is hurt. The soul is in the body. We live through our body. We live in life. But martyrs—no, mahatmas—have said that life is either larger or smaller than the universe. So, I want to tell you that life is greater than us. Because there is love and tenderness in it. I've been painfully caught in the snare of love.

How was it, my lord?

KING. I felt like weeping. There was no rhyme, rhythm or art in it. Goodness! I never knew you were so prosaic. Haven't the elders taught us to be poetic? Do you know how the dialogue should go? Listen to me—

I say: Beloved!

She says: My love!

I say: Oh, beloved! you are sitting on a chair in my heart. I may die, but I shall not let you get off.

She says: Oh, my love! Cupid is tossing me around like hay because you are not here. Don't be stubborn. Come to me.

I say: Oh, beloved, consoler of my heart, this life is joyous. Why stay apart? Let us be happy! Why shouldn't we be happy, lying and kissing in ten different styles on a bed of flowers? Tra, la, la, la!

How was it?

CHAMBERLAIN. Wonderful, my lord, just wonderful. But such a touching scene cannot be enacted in a garden.

KING. Why?

CHAMBERLAIN. There are too many mosquitoes at night. It will be very cold too. What if you swallow a mosquito when you are speaking? On the other hand, it'll be more spectacular if all this takes place in the travellers' bungalow.

KING. Do you think so? Then make arrangements in the travellers' bungalow as soon as you find the girl—the one in the green sari and blue blouse.

And listen, oh Chamberlain!
If you get that girl
bring her straightaway
to our travellers' bungalow!

CHAMBERLAIN. So be it, my lord!

SCENE THREE

The Ganesha temple. Samba and Shiva.

SHIVA. I've read so many stories and novels, but I've never come across any where that god's gift turns out to be a donkey. The only advantage is that now I have a job—waiting on a donkey.

SAMBA. You bastard, you don't understand a thing. You have a head, and god has given you a donkey. What more do you want? If you ask me, you could sell this donkey for at least a crore of rupees. Shall I show you how?

Hey, Ding Dong! (*Donkey brays.*)

Come here. (*Comes over.*)

Sit down. (*Sits.*)

Stand up. (*Stands.*)

Now, let's see you dance. (*Dances.*)

Shiva is very happy. Now they both dance with the donkey and sing.

SAMBA AND SHIVA. Salaam, Sir Ding Dong!
Great entertainer!
There is none to compare with you.
The King who rules this land is no tiger but a eunuch leopard.
You are better than him! Oh sir!
You walk on your forelegs, kick with your hindlegs—
twice two four,
you kick, walk and dance.

The King who rules this land is a mere two-legged man—
you are better than him.
Scriptures, knowledge, wisdom
stink like rotten garbage—
you eat it all and burp
and leave a mound of dung.
The King who rules this land has a head full of hayseed—you are better than him! Oh sir!

SAMBA. Now give me the sari and blouse. (*Shiva gives them to him*) What's this? A green sari and a blue blouse?

SHIVA. This was exactly what she was wearing.

SAMBA. So now you want me to look like her?

SHIVA. Aren't you my father?

SAMBA. Listen carefully! I'll need time between going into the house and getting the job. Don't make a fuss if I take time.

SHIVA. Right.

SAMBA. Don't start whistling if I'm late.

SHIVA. No.

SAMBA. I shall send the girl to you somehow. Until then, you must behave in a civilized manner. Do you understand?

SHIVA. I can't stay quiet for long. What shall I do?

SAMBA. Count your fingers and toes.

SHIVA. All right.

SAMBA. Remember, in their home my name is Bangari.

SCENE FOUR

Richman's house. Gajanimbe is standing by the window. Samba in green sari and blue blouse, i.e. Bangari, is standing near her.

GAJANIMBE. I cannot bear the pain of separation!

I cannot bear the love god's power,
No, no!
My dear love, why didn't you come?
You left me in the power of the love god.

My heart is burning in the flames of love's absence, since just the day before yesterday when that youth bewitched and stole my heart. Who will tell him that it is not right to leave a delicate girl like me victim of the love god's arrows? Without a glimpse of my lover, my mind is restless. Who will tell him that I am dying for lack of sleep? I toss and turn all night. Aha, there she comes. This woman is begging with outstretched hands for a servant's job in our house. I shall make her my confidante by persuading my mother to give her a job. Then with her help I shall catch that thief. (*Turns to Bangari*) You there! If you want the job, you'll have to wait till my mother comes. What did you say your name was?

SAMBA. Bangari.

GAJANIMBE. Are you from this town?

SAMBA. Yes.

GAJANIMBE. Bangari, do you see that boy standing in the backyard? Who is he? Do you know?

SAMBA (*to himself*). Oh, I see, my son has already put in his appearance. (*Aloud*) Yes, ma'am. He lives on our street.

GAJANIMBE. In your street? What is his name?

SAMBA. He is called Shiva. Why do you ask, ma'am?

GAJANIMBE. He has been standing there regularly for the past three days. There was an old man with him, too. He doesn't seem to be there today.

SAMBA. Was the old man good looking?

GAJANIMBE. Oh, no! He was like an old monkey. More or less like you. But the boy is terribly handsome. Don't you think so?

SAMBA. What do you mean, handsome? You couldn't sell him for two bidis. Look at his face, he can't even smile properly. But that other man, the one you said looks a little old, he is your true voluptuary. He's not all that old, either. How well he sings and dances! Do you know what people keep asking him? 'Sir, what is the secret of your youth?'

GAJANIMBE. He makes me want to puke, with his monkey face. Even you look better than him. But this young man! He's a real heartthrob.

SAMBA. But ma'am, he's a rascal. The other older man with him is a gentleman. This one can't even spit like him.

GAJANIMBE. If you admire the old man so much, why don't you go after him yourself? Why have come here? You won't get the job if you mention him again. Thank god the old fool is not here today.

SAMBA (*to himself*). Samba, this one is not for you. All these days, I thought my son was a fool. But he seems to have caused a stir in this girl's heart. Well done, my son, well done. Shiva, I admit at last that I am growing old.

GAJANIMBE. How old can he be?

SAMBA. Who? Me?

GAJANIMBE. Of course not! I mean the boy.

SAMBA. Forty or fifty perhaps.

GAJANIMBE. What is wrong with you? Speak properly or just get out.

SAMBA. I'm sorry ma'am. The boy is very young.

GAJANIMBE. Would you say he is a good boy?

SAMBA. He is a good boy, but the steps he takes . . .

GAJANIMBE. What is wrong with his steps? I saw him yesterday and he walks perfectly well. Did you say he's very good looking?

SAMBA. He is quite good looking, but the way he stands . . .

GAJANIMBE. Why? He is standing so smartly.

SAMBA. He's poor and he has a dirty face.

GAJANIMBE. But it's a lovely face, look!

SAMBA (*to himself*). Your game won't work any more, Samba. Shiva is rooted in her heart. (*Aloud*) That's all very well, ma'am. His behaviour, the way he stands, his face, his poverty—everything is pleasing. But the poor fellow has been struck by some disease for the past three days.

GAJANIMBE. Disease? For the past three days?

SAMBA. Yes. It seems he saw a beautiful girl. Since then he talks to himself, looks up at the sky, sighs, tosses and turns at night, sweats, shivers and quivers . . .

GAJANIMBE (*laughing*). Who is she?

SAMBA. She is from this very house.

GAJANIMBE. What? From this house? What's her name?

SAMBA. With her snake-like body
and her elephant-like gait,

Gajanimbe punishes
when asked for pleasure
that's what he says.

GAJANIMBE (*laughing*). A pack of lies!

SAMBA. Why should I lie, ma'am? It was he who sent me to you. He will die if you don't love him. I felt sorry to see the young lad dying unnecessarily, so I came. If you want that boy, find me a job in your house.

GAJANIMBE. Just wait till Mother comes. Oh, look. He is leaning on the donkey. He is stroking its back. Look, he is even putting his face near the donkey's and whispering something. How I wish I had been born that donkey! Bangari, do you think that worthless boy should do all that to a donkey? I haven't slept for three days, thinking of him, do you know?

SAMBA. You poor thing!

GAJANIMBE. Bangari, please call him names.

SAMBA. Why on earth, ma'am?

GAJANIMBE. If you do, perhaps I'll feel contemptuous towards him. Then I can sleep in peace.

SAMBA. Must I? Really?

GAJANIMBE. Go on. Go ahead.

SAMBA. Can you call him a man? He's a monkey and that's all there is to it. There are millions of monkeys in this world. What's so special about him? Choose another monkey, ma'am.

GAJANIMBE. But no other monkey will be so handsome.

SAMBA. Really ma'am! Look at his face. It's filthy.

GAJANIMBE. But isn't it handsome?

Godavari comes in.

GODAVARI. I've told you a thousand times not to stand by the window. If you stand there again to watch the street dogs, I shall break that dog's leg. Watch out!

SAMBA. She's a grown-up girl. She knows what to watch and what not to watch.

GODAVARI. She hasn't even grown wisdom teeth. How can you call her an adult? Anyway, who is this stranger?

GAJANIMBE. You wanted a maid. She has come to see you.

GODAVARI. Who needs a maid when there are two women as sturdy as rafters in the house? Forget it.

GAJANIMBE. You had asked for one yourself, remember?

GODAVARI. That was then. Now I don't need one.

GAJANIMBE. She's good worker, Mother. Keep her.

GODAVARI. Enough of your recommendations. How much do you want to be paid, woman?

SAMBA. Just ten rupees.

GODAVARI. Ten rupees! For how many years?

SAMBA. For a month.

GODAVARI. I doubt if even kings get paid so much. What kind of work will you do, anyway?

SAMBA. I'll wash, shine, sweep, spread the beds, eat, drink and sleep.

GODAVARI. Good heavens! Hold your tongue. If you want to work here, you must learn to keep quiet. Come! I'll show you what to do.

As *they start to go out, Richman comes in.*

RICHMAN. Would you believe it? There is a donkey standing outside that looks exactly like a horse.

GODAVARI. After looking at you, one hardly needs to look at a donkey.

RICHMAN. It's even better looking than me. Come and see.

They all go to the window and look.

GODAVARI. Yes, you're right! It sparkles. What ears! What legs! What a body!

RICHMAN. How wide, how long, how high, how deep!

GODAVARI. I've never seen a donkey like this till now! Where did you find it?

RICHMAN. Oh, come on. It's standing in the backyard. I just saw it.

GODAVARI. The boy who is standing there, who is he? (*The donkey brays. Samba and Gajanimbe make signs to each other*) How melodiously it brays!

RICHMAN. It's much better than the hymns you sing!

GODAVARI. Gajanimbe. Go and practise your music.

SAMBA. Why? Let her stand in the backyard and listen to the donkey's music. It's singing for free.

Gajanimbe slips out.

RICHMAN. Well, well, well! Who is this?

GODAVARI. The maid.

RICHMAN. Quite good looking. The nose is a bit . . .

SAMBA. I don't work with my nose. I use my hands.

GODAVARI. Listen, yesterday you were short of twelve paise. Did the accounts balance?

RICHMAN. Not yet, I still have to check them.

GODAVARI. Shut your loud mouth then, and go. You, woman, come with me.

They go out but come back again, walking backwards, and followed by the Chamberlain. He seems deliriously happy to see Samba. Samba and Godavari are frightened.

GODAVARI (*to Richman*). Look, there's somebody here.

CHAMBERLAIN. Green sari, blue blouse, green sari, blue blouse! (*Patting himself*) Well, Chamberlain, you've won at last, my son!

RICHMAN (*running up, scared*). Oh, the Chamberlain! Please come in, sir. Women, see to refreshments, bring plenty. Come on in, sir.

CHAMBERLAIN. Green sari, blue blouse! Wonderful!

RICHMAN. This is our . . .

CHAMBERLAIN. I know, I know!

RICHMAN. She came to us just today.

CHAMBERLAIN. I know all about you.

RICHMAN. I swear on my wife's feet, sir, I could never be a traitor. I don't even dream of such things.

GODAVARI. God help me! Was I not kissing the King's feet in my dream?

RICHMAN. Yes, indeed, I was with her too. I am witness to it, sir . . . and then didn't I lick his boots?

GODAVARI. Yes, yes.

RICHMAN. I have not subscribed to any revolution, sir. Green, Yellow, White, Red, any coloured bloc . . . I haven't paid a penny to any revolutionary.

CHAMBERLAIN. Good.

RICHMAN. That's not all. I have made sure that my friends don't pay either. These damned revolutionaries begged me for ten paise at least. Do you know what I said? You rascals, you won't get a penny even if I die. That's what I said, sir.

CHAMBERLAIN (*staring at Samba all the while, suddenly bursting into song like a romantic hero*).

I have seen, I have seen, I have seen the lovely maiden,
    and her intoxicating eyes!
Oh, the same green sari, the very same blue blouse!
Sari of green,
Blouse of blue,
Maiden of pale colour!
It is she, the one seen by the King!

Richman, do you know how much the King and I have talked of you?

GODAVARI. Of us?

CHAMBERLAIN (*pointing to Samba*). About this woman, to be exact.

RICHMAN. Oh, really? Don't get worried. No one's accusing you. On the contrary, good fortune is knocking at your door. What is your name, madam?

SAMBA. Bangari.

CHAMBERLAIN. But of course! It's not child's play to make the King's heart beat faster!

RICHMAN. Sir, would you mind explaining all this?

CHAMBERLAIN. What is there to explain? Take it for granted that the King feels entirely favourable towards you. Don't forget us later. That's all I ask.

RICHMAN. I don't understand . . .

CHAMBERLAIN. Oh, forget about it! That's just routine. I was the first one to tell the King about your daughter. Bangari, just watch! This house will be filled with gold.

RICHMAN. Sir, tell me what this is all about before I go mad!

CHAMBERLAIN. No, I shan't. What will you do?

RICHMAN. Oh my god!

GODAVARI (*imitating him*). Oh my god! Why don't you tell him straight? Chamberlain, this is not our daughter.

CHAMBERLAIN. Not your daughter?

GODAVARI. No. She's our maid.

CHAMBERLAIN (*shocked disgust in his eyes*). Stay by the window, you two. (*They go to Bangari*) Did you go to the garden for the Spring Festival the day before yesterday?

SAMBA (*lying to make use of the opportunity*). Yes, sir.

CHAMBERLAIN. Were you wearing the same sari, and the same blouse!

SAMBA. Yes, sir.

CHAMBERLAIN. Did anyone fall in love with you that day?

SAMBA. One? Two? There were a whole lot of people smitten by my beauty. How can I pick out one?

CHAMBERLAIN. Do you remember an elderly man casting loving glances at you?

SAMBA. Elderly? Yes. He had the bearing of a king.

CHAMBERLAIN (*happily*). And then?

SAMBA. He opened his mouth when he saw me and didn't shut it again. Has he shut it now, sir?

CHAMBERLAIN. Innocent girl! You don't realize what a big fish you've caught. The man who's had his mouth open since he saw you happens to be our King.

SAMBA (*as if in shock*). Ah! Ah!

GODAVARI (*looking out through the window*). Oh dear, that young man is talking to Gajanimbe and standing so close. Just look at him. Gajanimbe, be careful now!

CHAMBERLAIN. Why are you screaming? Keep quiet or else you'll rot in jail. (*Softly so that only Samba can hear*) Bangari, if you listen to me, I'll make your luck turn.

SAMBA. Did I say I wouldn't?

CHAMBERLINE. Tell me about yourself.

SAMBA. You ask me. Ask me if I'm married.

CHAMBERLAIN. Are you married?

SAMBA. Oh sir, if my husband had been alive, would I have been cast out into the streets like this? After he left this world, the street dogs started lifting their legs when they heard my name. Ask me why my husband died.

CHAMBERLAIN. Why did you husband die?

SAMBA. You are a nuisance! Why should he die? I killed him.

CHAMERLAIN. Why?

SAMBA. I was having an affair with the neighbour's husband. He found out. So I just hanged him to avoid unpleasantness. Aren't you going to ask me what I do for a living?

CHAMBERLAIN. What do you do for a living?

SAMBA. I was just about to tell you. I used to work for a fool. He was thin, tall and fair like you. Like you, he asked me what I could do. I said,

'I'll do whatever you tell me to (*pinching the Chamberlain's cheek*) but you must smile'. When I said that, he came forward, held my hand and asked, 'Bangari, can you make a bed?'

CHAMBERLAIN (*holding Samba's hand*). That's exactly what I'm asking you, Bangari. Can you make the King's bed?

RICHMAN. Sir, did you call?

GODAVARI. Oh, no! That boy is whispering something in Gajanimbe's ear. Look, look, he's biting her ears.

RICHMAN. Hey, Gajanimbe! Mind your earrings.

CHAMBERLAIN. Shut up! (*Only to Samba*) Bangari! You must lie to the King and say you are the Richman's daughter.

SAMBA. Of course.

GODAVARI. I must get three-quarters of what the King gives you.

SAMBA. You can keep the whole lot.

CHAMBERLAIN. Now and then you must tell the King whatever I tell you to.

SAMBA. Of course.

GODAVARI. He is embracing her and biting her cheeks. Hey, Gajanimbe!

CHAMBERLAIN (*shouts at her. To Samba*). It's all settled then?

SAMBA. Done! But we won't meet here. We'll meet at the Ganesha temple outside the city.

CHAMBERLAIN. At the Ganesha temple! Remember! (*Exit.*)

SCENE FIVE

Palace. King and Minister.

KING. Hey, Minister!

MINISTER. You called, my lord?

KING. I called to make sure whether you could hear me or not.

MINISTER. I can hear you, my lord, but I can hear the voice of the people even better.

KING. Tell me, Minister, how did the kings of yore begin their durbars?

MINISTER. They would call the Minister and ask about the welfare of the country.

KING. Oh yes, that's how Dharmaraya's durbar began in the play we saw the other day. Hey, Minister, are all our people content to sit and meditate with shut eyes on Shiva? Is our land blessed with plenty?

MINISTER. No, my lord. There is great discontent among the people.

KING. The minister in the play didn't speak like this.

MINISTER. You are not the king in a play. Nor is this a play either. You are a real king. You must pay attention to the genuine pain of real people.

KING. Of course, I do. Speak up.

MINISTER. My lord, I'm younger than you in years.

KING. And in intelligence too!

MINISTER. I must tell you some unpleasant truths for the welfare of the country. Pardon me.

KING. You are forgiven but you spit more than you speak. White Elephant has told me that the sun rises and sets regularly on our land. Is that right?

MINISTER. My lord, taxes have become a great burden. Thieves and murderers abound. There is drought in the land and corruption everywhere.

KING. If all this is true, who do you think is responsible? It just shows that you haven't been doing your job well.

MINISTER. That is not true, my lord. Neither you nor White Elephant realize our difficulties. It will be dangerous if you don't wake up in time. The people are getting together and talking of revolution.

KING. Revolution? Have we ourselves not engineered a few revolutions through the government?

MINISTER. The government?

KING. Yes. Green revolution, white revolution, yellow revolution. Who was responsible for all these?

MINISTER. I lack the sense of humour to laugh at your witticisms, my lord. I cannot be blind to the agony of the people and the insolence of officials. Please listen to me—even now . . .

KING. What's all this? Do you think you are big enough to preach to me?

MINISTER. I am certainly not preaching, my lord. I am just trying to make you understand that this is a state of emergency. All the signs of a revolution are visible. Your end . . .

KING. Really! How should I react when the slippers on my feet tell me what to do?

MINISTER. You'll take them off and throw them away, won't you? Here, accept my resignation. (*Walks off.*)

KING. Damn you, you bastard!

SERVANT (*enters*). My lord! White Elephant is here.

KING. Let him in.

Servant goes out.

WHITE ELEPHANT (*as he enters*). Victory to you, my lord.

KING. How can it be? I believe people are dissatisfied, ready for a revolution? If I ask you, you say everything is all right.

WHITE ELEPHANT. Sir, don't be upset. I shall whisper in your ear what our spies have just learnt. Please lend me your ear.

KING. There you are. Out with it.

WHITE ELEPHANT. My lord, according to the reports, the Minister is the leader of the revolution.

KING. What?

WHITE ELEPHANT. Yes, my lord. We found out that he has his eye on your throne. We all felt sorry for him and proud of you.

KING. Listen, White Elephant. Can't you send that Minister to prison on some pretext or the other?

WHITE ELEPHANT. Why do you need a pretext, my lord? Am I not here to fulfil your desires? Don't worry. He will go to prison today. Do you know what one of his followers said in a speech the other day? 'How many bungalows does each White Elephant own?' That's what he said. Should anyone say such a thing?

KING. Of course . . .

WHITE ELEPHANT. My lord, because there are people like this, there is a king like you. Because there are kings like you, there are officials like us. Because there are officials like us, this country is what it is. If we weren't here, would the country be like this, my lord? You are a king and you have a palace. We are your servants—shouldn't we have at least a couple of small bungalows each?

KING. I believe there were once huts where you built your bungalows.

WHITE ELEPHANT. That's called progress, my lord. We have a bungalow where there was a hut. We are the direct descendants of the slaves of the Queen of London. That's why we are called the I.A.S.

KING. That's all right. What's the purpose of your present visit?

WHITE ELEPHANT. My lord, theft cases have increased in the country. According to the latest M.Y.G. Report, out of four crores, three crores ninety-nine lakhs ninety-nine thousand nine hundred and ninety-nine people are thieves.

KING. Who is the one left out? Me?

WHINE ELEPHANT. Most certainly, my lord.

KING. That means you are a thief too.

WHITE ELEPHANT. There is a slight alteration in the figures, my lord. The last digits are nine hundred and ninety-eight. If you care to peruse . . .

KING. That means you are not a thief either. What next?

WHITE ELEPHANT. It is a sin to steal. But no one stops stealing for that reason. Why should we try to shake off something that has become a custom?

KING. What do you mean?

WHITE ELEPHANT. My lord, how about giving licenses for stealing?

KING. Excellent.

WHITE ELEPHANT. If we fix a government rate for each license, everyone will procure one. The treasury will overflow . . .

KING. Yes . . . What's the noise outside?

WHITE ELEPHANT. Everyone is waiting outside to buy the license. Please sign quickly, my lord.

SERVANT (*enters*). My lord, Small Change is waiting outside.

KING. I shall sign later. Wait. Send Small Change in.

Servant goes out.

WHITE ELEPHANT. Be careful of Small Change, my lord. He is definitely not trustworthy. Just say something insignificant and send him away. Another thing, my lord. I believe the Minister has resigned. Is that true? Not that it matters. I am around to look after things. I shall wait outside, my lord. (*White Elephant goes out. On the way he whispers to Small Change*) Greetings! I've spoken well of you before the King.

SMALL CHANGE. Thank you, sir. (*Coming forward*) May victory be yours, O King!

KING. It's my ears you want, isn't it?

SMALL CHANGE. Yes, my lord.

KING. Alas, if my ears were a yard long, how easy it would be to give them to you! I could have stuffed one of my ears into each of your mouths and gone to sleep.

SMALL CHANGE. Your ears have already grown a span from giving them generously to us when we ask for them.

KING. Really? Let them grow even longer. Anyway, tell me what you have to say.

SMALL CHANGE. Has the Minister resigned, my lord? If he has, please accept his resignation. I am here to look after things. But you must be careful of White Elephant. He's not trustworthy. He's the treacherous kind.

KING. What is the noise I hear outside?

SMALL CHANGE. The artists are singing your praises, my lord.

KING. Why?

SMALL CHANGE. Because you are going to sign the letter I'm about to show you. That's why.

KING. What does the letter say?

SMALL CHANGE. My lord, your concern for the poor is renowned in the whole capital. Your aim is to uplift the poor and keep them happy. Is that not so, my lord?

KING. Yes, most certainly.

SMALL CHANGE. Here, my lord. I have a project for keeping the poor smiling. Please sign, my lord.

KING. First explain.

SMALL CHANGE. It's like this, my lord. Gather all the poor together in a field.

KING. And then give a speech?

SMALL CHANGE. No, no. The greatest actors in the country will go there with baskets. Baskets full of bread. Then they will eat it in front of the poor. 'Delicious,' they will say. The poor will cry out at them angrily, hungrily—suffering. These people will keep on eating and the others will just keep on watching and watching and watching. In the end, they will notice that the bread is made of cardboard! Cardboard bread being eaten like real bread! The poor people will clap and shout happily.

KING. The poor people will laugh?

SMALL CHANGE. I've tried it, my lord.

KING. Did they really laugh?

SMALL CHANGE. Yes indeed, my lord. They were falling about laughing. Some fell and never got up. All the poor people were laughing as if they had just come out of a lunatic asylum. When I looked to see why, I could see the actors eating mud in the same way as they had eaten cardboard bread, and the poor people kept on laughing.

KING. That is a very good plan. Blessed is this land that has officers like you. What brains you have! Our people are not worthy even to pimp for you.

Noise increases outside. Servant runs in.

SERVANT. My lord, people have gathered outside and are demanding to see you.

White Elephant comes in.

WHITE ELEPHANT. They are citizens, my lord. They want to congratulate you when you authorize the license for stealing. Please sign quickly. my lord.

SMALL CHANGE. They are not just citizens, my lord. Artists have gathered together to congratulate you after you sign the bill.

Servant goes out.

WHITE ELEPHANT. Citizens have gathered outside.

SMALL CHANGE. Artists have gathered outside.

WHITE ELEPHANT. I know how much I've taken to get the bill passed.

Servant runs in again.

SERVANT. My lord, everyone is shouting 'Victory to the Revolution'.

WHITE ELEPHANT. They won't keep quiet if the artists' bill is passed.

SMALL CHANGE. Whoever heard of giving licenses for stealing!

WHITE ELEPHANT (*to Small Change*). Why on earth are we betraying each other? We officials are all one, aren't we? If kings have isms, we also have our proletarianism (*Winks*).

KING. What did you say?

WHITE ELEPHANT. There is some meaning in their call for revolution, my lord. Giving licenses for stealing, redeeming people through art—all this is revolutionary thinking. That's why people are craving revolution.

KING. Is our ex-Minister there?

SERVANT. He is trying to calm the people, my lord. But no one can hear him.

The noise is increasing. Slogans heard—'Victory to the revolution', etc.

SMALL CHANGE. Good god! It *is* a revolution! The Minister is behind all this. Hey, you there!

SERVANT. Yes, sir?

SMALL CHANGE. Set the police on the people. It is the King's order.

SERVANT. As you command, sir. (*Goes out.*)

Noises, the sound of lathi charge, tear gas.

WHITE ELEPHANT. Who is there?

SERVANT (*comes in*). Yes, sir?

WHITE ELEPHANT. Set the army on the people, tell them to shoot at sight. It is the King's order.

SEVANT. As you command, sir. (*Goes out.*)

Noise of shooting is added to the previous noises.

WHITE ELEPHANT. My lord. I don't think we can quell this uprising. It will be better if we run away from here.

Servant runs in.

SERVANT. Please don't go, my lord. There are people everywhere. They have sworn not to go away unless they see your face.

KING. My face? I haven't washed it since I got up this morning. How can I show them my stale face?

SERVANT. But they won't go away until they see your face, my lord. That's sure.

KING. Very well, then. If my subjects insist on seeing my face, there is nothing I can do. However, I washed my feet after going to the bogs in the morning. Couldn't I show them my feet instead?

WHITE ELEPHANT. That should do, my lord.

SMALL CHANGE. It won't do, my lord.

WHITE ELEPHANT. It would be enough.

SMALL CHANGE. No, it wouldn't.

WHITE ELEPHANT. Look, you are inexperienced. Learn to respect senior officers.

SMALL CHANGE. Experience? Even a donkey has experience.

WHITE ELEPHANT. Who are you calling a donkey? Your father was one and so was your mother!

SMALL CHANGE. And your grandmother and grandfather . . .

KING. Hey, you dogs!

Both are quiet.

WHITE ELEPHANT. It'll be enough if you show one foot, my lord.

SMALL CHANGE. It won't be, my lord. The people are asking with great devotion. You must show both feet at least.

KING. Since I haven't been endowed with another two legs, let's just show the two I do possess. (*He leans on the two officers and sticks his legs out through the window.*)

Noise continues outside. The King speaks to a servant.

Go and tell them that my face is dirty, so they must be content with the sight of my feet today.

Servant goes out.

KING. My feet have become wet.

SMALL CHANGE. They are probably washing your feet and worshipping you, my lord.

KING. The water is warm. Could someone possibly be pissing? (*As the noise continues, the King's feet are beaten*) Oh god! Someone's thrashing me. Pull in my feet, quickly . . . quickly.

SMALL CHANGE. Isn't it wrong to pull in your feet without a government order?

KING. I'm ordering you to pull.

WHITE ELEPHANT. This man objects to everything. You convince him first, my lord.

KING. Oh dear! They are pulling from that side. My feet, my poor feet! They'll come off.

WHITE ELEPHANT. I'll look after the government order. Pull! We won't let go even if your legs break off. Pull, my lord, pull harder.

The King is being pulled both ways. No one is giving in. Meanwhile, Shiva comes running in, shouting.

SHIVA. Your Highness! If you give me a chance, I can get rid of all the people outside in one minute.

KING. Do whatever you can, quickly.

SHIVA (*shouts*). Ding Dong! (*Fierce braying is heard from outside*) Ding Dong! Is it not our duty to save the King? (*More braying*) In that case, kick all the people outside.

Now there is a change in the noise coming from outside. The donkey's braying becomes loud and fierce. Sounds of kicking and people screaming. In a short while, the King's legs are freed. The King and others look out of the window and watch the donkey's activities with joy and admiration.

KING. Good heavens! Is this a horse, a donkey or a demon?

SMALL CHANGE. Look at the way it chases and kicks people. This is a godly animal, my lord.

WHITE ELEPHANT. The lady in England has three or four like this.

SMALL CHANGE. See how all the people have run away! And the donkey is chasing them and kicking.

WHITE ELEPHANT. Great, great! What a name! Ding Dong!

KING. Ding Dong!

WHITE ELEPHANT. It was I who sent for this donkey boy, my lord.

KING. Ding Dong!

SMALL CHANGE. This donkey boy works in my house, my lord.

KING. Ding Dong! Excellent. What is your name, little one?

SHIVA. My name is Shiva. I am a poor man, my lord. If you would kindly give me a job, I could make a living.

WHITE ELEPHANT. Yes, indeed. I recommend that he be made the Chairman of the Wildlife Preservation Committee.

SMALL CHANGE. Certainly not. Make him the President of the Domestic Animal Board, my lord.

KING. Shiva! Go and fetch your Ding Dong.

Shiva goes out and comes back with Ding Dong. Everyone is astounded at the sight of the donkey.

KING. A miracle, a miracle! How beautifully built! Its legs, its ears! I wish I had ears like that!

WHITE ELEPHANT. I wish I had four legs like Ding Dong too!

SMALL CHANGE. If I had been born on a Sunday instead of a Saturday, I might have been born as Ding Dong.

KING. Listen everybody! From today the prime minister of this country is . . .

WHITE ELEPHANT. Prime Minister Shivanna!

EVERYONE EXCEPT THE KING. Hail, hail!

KING. Listen carefully. From today the prime minister of this nation is not Shivanna but Ding Dong!

WHITE ELEPHANT. Your Highness!

KING. All of you say 'Hail to Ding Dong'.

ALL. Hail, hail!

KING. Ding Dong is the prime minister. Shiva is his P.A. Listen, Shiva, you are to look after the prime minister and translate his desires for us. The palace in the park is yours. Understand? Servant, take them to the palace and organize everything. Write down the new orders. (*Goes in*.)

The Chamberlain can be heard proclaiming the orders from the wings. White Elephant and Small Change write them down.

CHAMBERLAIN. (a) Nobody will call Ding Dong saheb a donkey any longer, nor will they criticize him. If anyone does so, in mind or words, he will be imprisoned for six months and charged a penalty of Rs 10,000. From now on, instead of using god's name in greeting, everyone must say Ding Dong.

(b) People will especially remember the way in which the honourable Ding Dong saheb saved the King's life by driving away the revolutionaries. Everyone will respectfully buy the special postage stamp issued in his honour.

(c) Grass from Australia, oilseed from America, fodder from China and waste paper from England will be imported for the honourable Ding Dong saheb. For this, the people will start paying, as from today, a special fodder tax to the King's treasury. Over.

SMALL CHANGE. Sir, Mr Shivanna, there is no mention of arrangements for the nights. Is Ding Dong saheb married?

SHIVA. No.

SMALL CHANGE. In that case, shouldn't arrangements be made for a *ship-fish* at night?

SHIVA. What do you mean? Ship-fish?

SMALL CHANGE. We have two white she-donkeys, both of the right age. No venereal disease. We have a doctor's certificate. I shall have the bill passed if you let me know your percentage. If this doesn't suit you, we have a very young brown mare. A virgin. You may test it if you want. If you are agreeable to fifty-fifty, I shall bring it over. Come to Mantralaya Bar in the evening. I shall be waiting . . . (*Goes out*.)

WHITE ELEPHANT. Ding Dong, Shivanna.

SHIVA. Ding Dong, sir.

WHITE ELEPHANT. Honestly speaking, I don't think it is right to insult Ding Dong saheb by supplying him with donkeys and mares. He may accept what you give him just out of good manners. But think, if we give donkeys and mares to the prime minister, where will the King's reputation be? What about our own for that matter? If you say yes, I know of girls who are prepared to come. Shall I send for them? In any case, come to Balaji Bar in the evening . . . (*Goes out*.)

SCENE SIX

Ganesha temple. Samba comes in singing, with a newspaper in his hand. A man is sitting in the corner, drinking. Samba does not notice him.

SAMBA. Times have changed.
A poisonous wind blows through the land.
Iron floats and cork sinks.
Buddha, Basava, Yenkanani—they are all here.
The more you slide, the longer the road.
They sing his praises,
'Ding Dong, Ding Dong,' they call.
Man and woman dance like donkeys on all fours,
wearing borrowed faces,
feeling to see if the wise have grown tails.
They tie gods to donkeys' tails.
They are burping from the fake they're fed.
They sing his praises,
'Ding Dong, Ding Dong,' they call.

My god, these people are really mad. Read any newspaper, nothing but Ding Dong. Talk to anyone, nothing but Ding Dong! Let me see if there's anything special today. (*Turns the pages over*) Ding Dong's statue on D.G.K. Road . . . smuggling of she-donkeys . . . blood donation from Ding Dong Fans Association. King's assurance about increase in the fodder tax . . . consumers warned . . .

It may have come to your notice that many firms are manufacturing Ding Dong talcum powder. But there is only one government concern which makes use of genuine Ding Dong droppings, the others are using dung from inferior animals. Thus cheating the public. A government spokesman has warned the public about this fraud. Excellent.

BIRAYYA. What's so great about that? Do you know that college girls write love letters to Ding Dong?

SAMBA (*to himself*). Just look at him, drinking alone. I feel as if I've seen him somewhere.

BIRAYYA. Do you know what one of the girls has written? It seems she dreamt that she was at the disco, dancing with Ding Dong.

SAMBA. That's all very well, but while dancing, did Ding Dong lose two legs or did she grow two more?

BIRAYYA. I'm not the kind who'd steal into another person's dream. Look at me—tell me if I seem to be that kind of thief! Do you know how dear fodder and oilseed have become?

SAMBA. Why? Have people started eating oilseed?

BIRAYYA. What else? It now costs three rupees a plate in hotels.

SAMBA. Well, well. I have known lots of different people. I know of people who eat roti without vegetables or rice without curry. But I hadn't heard of people who live on oilseed even though they can get vegetables and curry.

BIRAYYA. I've told them it isn't food. But they say this is the way to succeed in life.

SAMBA. Isn't there anyone who can give them the right advice?

BIRAYYA. There is one pundit among us. He talks only about books. His mouth is open even while he sleeps. Whenever he opens his mouth, he talks about books. He has never talked about rice and curry. He talks about books while mice eat his share of rice and curry. They've grown fat with all they eat, and he has become as thin as a stick. When we ask him why, he says his name is 'Pundit'.

SAMBA. Uh, you make me laugh. I dreamt of someone last night. He was like a young fish.

BIRAYYA. Really? Who was he?

SAMBA. I can't remember. Maybe it was you . . .

BIRAYYA. You can call me a fish, you can call me a crocodile. Of all the people who have talked to me recently, you are the only one I can understand.

SAMBA. It was just a dream. Don't worry about it. Anyway, I see you're drinking. You don't have the culture to ask me if I'd like some too.

BIRAYYA. Do you want my culture or my drink?

SAMBA. Drink.

BIRAYYA. Then shut your arse and listen to me. Politics means making speeches. If you hit the table when you speak, it's establishment politics. If you hit the air, it's revolution. Our leader—the bookworm—used to speak hitting out at the air. Do you know what about? About books, about revolution in books. I was wild with myself. Do you know why? For listening to it with my mouth and my arse shut. I kicked myself in my mind.

SAMBA. Good. You did well. You should have kicked him in your mind too.

BIRAYYA. How can one be frank at all times?

SAMBA. True, true. You still look like a fish to me, but I can't say so. I must call you Indra, Chandra or else I won't get my drink.

BIRAYYA. That's the way to get on. In my opinion, our leader is no god. What do you say? He's only human. Do you know why . . .

SAMBA (*angrily*). I don't want to talk. I want a drink. Will you give me one or not?

BIRAYYA. No, I won't. Shall I tell you something else?

SAMBA. No. Just shut up.

BIRAYYA. You didn't tell me your dream . . .

SAMBA. What dream?

BIRAYYA. You said you saw me in a dream—that one.

SAMBA. Give me a drink and I'll tell you.

BIRAYYA. Why only a drink? I'll give you my life. Tell me about the dream first.

SAMBA. Only if you give me a drink.

BIRAYYA. No. People who drink give speeches about books. I get bored stiff.

SAMBA. I need a drink to free my tongue.

BIRAYYA. It's a pity you talk like our leader (*Weeps*).

SAMBA. Good heavens! What happened to make you cry?

BIRAYYA. Tell me why I shouldn't cry. I'm sad because there is no one who cares about my opinion of this city. I hoped you might listen to me, but even you only want a drink.

SAMBA. I will ask you your opinion. Will you give me a drink?

BIRAYYA. There you are! (*Gives him the drink. After Samba has drunk his fill*) Ask me now.

SAMBA. What's your opinion of this city?

BIRAYYA (*excited*). This city is a sewage tank. In the beginning it was a river. Now they have built a dam around it and made it into a tank. There is a forest around it. 'Forest' means an area where there is a thick growth of trees and shrubs. But the forest I'm talking about has no such growth. What else is there then? Just thorn bushes and thorn trees. There are fruits hanging from these thorn trees. Thief! Do you want to eat them? You go near, but you no longer see fruits. They are human skulls. How do you like that?

SAMBA (*excited too*). Brother, you are talking about the first half of my dream. After you run away, scared at the sight of the skulls, I go there. The skulls are clapping and laughing when I come. I look around to see why. There is a hefty fisherman catching little fishes in the tank and swallowing them whole. I catch a little fish too. When I put it on the table to cut it, it starts to sing.

Save my life,
do me a favour—
I'll give you the sun,
please break the dam!

BIRAYYA. And then?

SAMBA. I hadn't seen its eyes till then. As I kept looking at it, I got scared and woke up. It has eyes just like yours.

BIRAYYA. No! You did wrong to wake up so soon.

SAMBA. If I see the fish in my dream asking me to break down the dam with a pick and axe, I *will* break it down. Do you know why? I can't bear to see the little fishes die.

BIRAYYA. That's not all, brother. You can't do that job alone. I'll be sleeping with my pick and crowbar beside me. You must call me too.

SAMBA. What shall I call you?

BIRAYYA. Just say Birayya. That's enough. Here, drink some more. Sleep well. May the same dream come back. I'll come back soon.

SAMBA. Where are you going, brother?

BIRAYYA. To fetch the pick and crowbar. Remember, you have sown the seed in my mind. For you it is just a seed. But I can already see the fruit.

I shall give you the sun—
break the dam . . .

Goes off singing.

SCENE SEVEN

King and Chamberlain in the palace.

KING. Why are you looking so happy?

CHAMBERLAIN. I have no reason to weep, sir.

KING. How many reasons do you want? A hundred? A thousand?

CHAMBERLAIN. Give me just two, my lord. That will be enough.

KING. Shut up! It's because of worthless fellows like you that all this is happening.

CHAMBERLAIN. But, my lord . . .

KING. Shut your mouth! (*Chamberlain puts his hand over his mouth*) Tell me whether I can get angry or not.

CHAMBERLAIN. You asked me to shut my mouth, my lord.

KING. Never mind. You may talk with your mouth shut.

CHAMBERLAIN. What shall I say?

KING. Whether I can get angry or not.

CHAMBERLAIN. You are angry, my lord.

KING. There is a reason for my anger.

CHAMBERLAIN. You can get angry.

KING. Do you know how angry I am?

CHAMBERLAIN. No, my lord.

KING. I'm angry in two places! Ask me why.

CHAMBERLAIN. Why?

KING. I made that Ding Dong donkey the prime minister because he saved my life. Now look at the fame he has won in this country. His name is on everyone's lips. Everyone is singing songs about him. Hymns to him! Do they ever think of me or remember that their king's name is Kalmadi? Now tell me if I shouldn't be angry in the head.

CHAMBERLAIN. Of course, of course. And where else are you angry?

KING. You want to know? You promised to bring that girl. Where is she? How long can I be expected to wait? I'm angry below the belt, too.

CHAMBERLAIN. You've every reason to be angry, my lord. But you are a generous man, and if you will lend me your ears, as you do every day, I can pacify you in both places.

KING. Go ahead.

CHAMBERLAIN. My lord, your minister Ding Dong saheb is now a shining star! In the heads of intellectuals, in the hearts of young girls, in the eyes of old men, in the sky of our land he is twinkling away.

KING. Yes.

CHAMBERLAIN. My lord, when do such twinkling stars turn into charcoal?

KING. When?

CHAMBERLAIN. When they get married, of course. Get Ding Dong saheb married.

KING. Bravo, Chamberlain! You too have become an intellectual. I'm sure all this is thanks to me.

Who's there?

SERVANT (*enters*). What do you command, my lord?

KING. Go and call White Elephant.

SERVANT. As you command, my lord. (*Goes out*.)

KING. Chamberlain! Let's get that Ding Dong donkey married off, but not to a donkey. Let it be to a beautiful girl. Ding Dong is a donkey after all. If we get him married, his wife will eventually be mine. What do you think of my idea?

CHAMBERLAIN. Wonderful, my lord!

WHITE ELEPHANT (*enters*). My lord, did you call me?

KING. White Elephant. Arrange a wedding for Ding Dong—the kind where they choose their own bridegroom, a *swayamvara*. Those who wish to may bring their girls. But the choice is Ding Dong's alone. Do you understand?

WHITE ELEPHANT. Yes, sir. But this won't be a *swayamvara*. Since it is Ding Dong saheb who is choosing his own bride, it is a *swayamvadhu*.

KING. All right. Let it be proclaimed throughout the country that there is to be a ceremony—a *swayamvadhu* for Ding Dong.

WHITE ELEPHANT. As you say, my lord. (*Goes out.*)

KING. Well, Chamberlain. That's the end of the Ding Dong affair. The anger of the head has cooled down. Now what about the anger below the belt? Actually, that is stronger.

CHAMBERLAIN. That anger, really speaking, is without reason, my lord.

KING. What do you mean?

CHAMBERLAIN. I have already seen the girl you mentioned, my lord.

KING (*excited*). You actually saw her?

CHAMBERLAIN. With my own eyes, my lord.

KING. What is she like?

CHAMBERLAIN. Need you ask, my lord? She is a doll, a doll . . .

KING. Isn't she breathtakingly beautiful?

CHAMBERLAIN. The loveliest in the whole world! Her eyes are like jasmine, her ears like champak, her lips like guava. There is nothing I can compare her face to.

KING. Is she really all that beautiful? Then?

CHAMBERLAIN. Do you know what we talked about?

KING. About me? What did you say?

CHAMBERLAIN. Our King—how good, how dignified, how valiant, how heroic . . .

KING. Did she say that?

CHAMBERLAIN. No, I did.

KING. What did she say?

CHAMBERLAIN. She just listened.

KING. Then didn't you say anything?

CHAMBERLAIN. Wait, Wait! I'm coming to that. She is *madly* in love with you . . .

KING. Madly. Did she say anything about my age?

CHAMBERLAIN. Looking at you, people wonder if you are old enough be married yet.

KING. Is that so? Is that how I look?

CHAMBERLAIN. Looking at you, I would say you are twenty or fifteen.

KING. Did her parents think it would be a mismatch?

CHAMBERLAIN. Never, sir. Let me tell you the truth. The family seems to be inclined towards elderly men. Amitabh Bachchan, Dev Anand—you don't see any of these youngsters in their house. On the contrary, it's full of pictures of Janaka, Bhishma, Gandhi, Tolstoy, Vyasa, Durvasa—all men of a certain age.

KING. Really? That's wonderful. It shows how cultivated they are.

CHAMBERLAIN. It would have been the same with me if I had been born a woman. I wouldn't have looked at boys. I'd just have been interested in elderly men like you. What do youngsters have, anyway?

KING. You are right. I don't understand why these wretched girls long for young men.

CHAMBERLAIN. But then, my lord, it is only young girls from the lower classes who are like that. Girls from good families always look at older men, especially men like you, because you are cultivated.

KING. You would say that?

CHAMBERLAIN. What else could I say, my lord? Look at your build, your gait, your way of sitting, your way of getting up, your way of falling down. Do you have any shortcomings at all?

KING. Well. Once in a while, I suffer a little from asthma. That's about all.

CHAMBERLAIN Oh, that's nothing. You look so handsome when you have an attack of asthma.

KING. What's her name?

CHAMBERLAIN. Her name is Bangari.

KING. A lovely name! When will she come?

CHAMBERLAIN. Now.

KING. No, no! Bring the royal physician first.

CHAMBERLAIN. Your health is quite good, my lord.

KING. I'm quite well, but I'd like to be healthier in certain parts. Let's have the programme tomorrow night. Make it in the travellers' bungalow. I shall come at ten o'clock. Everything must be properly arranged. Tell White Elephant and Small Change about it. If anything goes wrong, no one will be forgiven! (*Goes out.*)

CHAMBERLAIN. Who is there?

SERVANT (*enters*). Yes, sir?

CHAMBERLAIN. Call White Elephant. (*He comes in.*)

Look here, White Elephant, a guest of our King will be coming tomorrow night. Make proper arrangements at the travellers' bungalow.

Chamberlain goes out. White Elephant presses the desk bell he takes out of his pocket and Small Change comes in.

WHITE ELEPHANT. Listen! A guest of the King will be staying at the travellers' bungalow. Make sure proper arrangements are made.

White Elephant goes out. Small Change presses the desk bell he takes out of his pocket. It makes no sound, so he carries it inside.

SCENE EIGHT

Travellers' bungalow. Samba and Shiva. Samba is dressing up as a woman. Shiva is looking on in wonder. Servant is waiting outside.

SHIVA. If you ask me, the sooner we leave this town the better. I'm scared to see you playing around with the King, White Elephant and the Chamberlain.

SAMBA. What is there to be scared about? Play the game. If you win, you get the woman. If you lose, what do you lose? The donkey's tail. If Ganesha's boon proves false, then he's in trouble. Don't get worked up about all this. Give me that pearl. Did you meet Gajanimbe?

SHIVA. Yes.

SAMBA. What did she say?

SHIVA. What else? Her mother was telling her to go to the *swayamvara*—no, *swayamvadhu*—celebration. She was even threatening to carry her there by force if she wouldn't go.

SAMBA. That's fine.

SHIVA. What do you mean? She was being stubborn and saying she'd rather die than marry a donkey.

SAMBA. Then what?

SHIVA. I wanted to suggest a way out, but that old woman never left her side. In the end, I did manage to tell her that she should come and I'd make the donkey choose her. She'd be married in name to a donkey, but I would still be around.

SAMBA. Do you think she'll come tomorrow for the *swayamvadhu* celebration?

SHIVA. She said she'd come but I'd be responsible if anything went wrong. I agreed, so she'll come. Father, why are you dressing up as a woman?

SAMBA. This is the fun of the game, son. Everybody is either putting on makeup or taking it off. With a little makeup, a donkey becomes a king. Take it off, and a king becomes a donkey. A woman becomes a man and a man turns into a woman . . . I think Small Change is here. Have a look.

SHIVA. I'm scared, Father. May I leave?

SAMBA. Wait. I will entertain you well.

Small Change comes in at the other side of the stage.

SMALL CHANGE. Who is that?

SERVANT. Ding Dong, sir.

SMALL CHANGE. I believe somebody has arrived?

SERVANT. Ding Dong saheb's P.A. is inside, sir.

SMALL CHANGE. Who? Shiva?

SERVANT. Yes. There is someone else with him.

SMALL CHANGE. Is there? (*Coming closer and whispering*) Man or woman?

SERVANT. Man, sir.

SMALL CHANGE. What is he to our boss? To the boss?

SERVANT. Nothing at all, sir. He is not an important person. He looks like a tramp.

SMALL CHANGE. So you think he is some common person? Then perhaps our boss' guest hasn't arrived yet. Never mind. Tell Shiva that the second-in-charge is here. Ask him to come out.

Servant goes out.

SHIVA (*coming out*). Greetings, sir.

SMALL CHANGE. Ding Dong! The boss said somebody important was coming. Is he here?

SHIVA. No one important has arrived. There is only a woman here.

SMALL CHANGE. A woman? I was told it was a man. What does she look like?

SHIVA. Quite beautiful. She said she wanted a room.

SMALL CHANGE. Worthless fellow! What were you doing inside alone?

SHIVA. Nothing. She wanted to know where the toilet was. I was showing her.

SMALL CHANGE (*to himself*). Oh, I see. White Elephant is up to something after scaring me into believing it was someone important. Well, well. (*Aloud*) Who are you to show her the toilet? Am I not here? Be off! Ding Dong must be hungry. Feed him.

Shiva goes out. Small Change goes in.

SAMBA (*looking at him*). Oh, oh! I'm so happy to see you. I can't tell you how happy I am to see you. I'm . . . I'm very, very happy. Aren't you?

SMALL CHANGE (*dismayed*). What did you say?

SAMBA. Aren't you happy too?

SMALL CHANGE. No.

SAMBA. Oh dear! I wish you were.

SMALL CHANGE. What?

SAMBA. You know, happy.

SMALL CHANGE. Why?

SAMBA. Because it's good for a man to be happy. Good health, good appetite, good shitting . . .

SMALL CHANGE. Maybe.

SAMBA. That would have been nice.

SMALL CHANGE. What would have been nice?

SAMBA. If you'd been happy.

SMALL CHANGE. Oh. Who are you? Are you related to the boss?

SAMBA. Please come in, won't you?

SMALL CHANGE. Who are you? Why have you come here?

SAMBA. I believe there is an attendant's job in Small Change's office.

SMALL CHANGE. Yes. There is a vacancy.

SAMBA. I asked White Elephant to get me that job and he told me to come here. So I came.

SMALL CHANGE. Well, I never! Fancy him trying to find a job for her in my office . . . What's your name?

SAMBA. Sundari.

SAMBA. Look here, Sundari. That White Elephant is a good-for-nothing loafer. He has lied to you. Don't be taken in by such people.

SAMBA. Goodness! The things he promised. Anyway it was good I came. I have met a god-like person in you. Please help me to get that job, sir.

SMALL CHANGE. Who knows how many young girls that rascal has cheated. What did you say your name was? Sundari? Nice name. Come here. There's something you don't know. The King listens only to me. Do you know what he said the other day? The big boss is stupid. Give him a kick. 'How could I, my lord?' I asked. Do you know what His

Highness did? He said, 'Like this,' and kicked me in the arse! (*Laughs happily*.)

SAMBA. My! Are you really that intimated with the King? Then please tell the King and find me a job, sir.

SMALL CHANGE. Why the King? I'm here. He won't change even a letter of what I write. I'm the one who writes down all the King's orders, do you know that?

SAMBA. In that case you are my only hope. Please get me the job.

SMALL CHANGE. Leave it to me. If I get you the job, I expect the usual . . . er . . . you know what. What do you say? (*Shuts the door*.)

SAMBA. Don't you worry about that. I am only concerned that the big boss might arrive before I can give it to you. That's all.

SMALL CHANGE. What if he does come? Do you think I'm scared of him? I don't care. I wouldn't move an inch even if his grandfather came. What does he think I am?

SAMBA. In that case, why waste time? Come and accept my services.

SMALL CHANGE. Services?

SAMBA. Is it right of you, O, love god,
this cruelty to me, a woman?
Is it right to take aim
and shoot whizz whizz
your arrows at my heavy breasts?

SMALL CHANGE. O, Sundari, I lay my heart at your feet!

There is a knock on the door before they can embrace.

SAMBA. Who is that?

VOICE FROM OUTSIDE. The big boss is here. Open the door.

SMALL CHANGE. Oh god! The big boss.

SAMBA. I will say, 'The little boss is here. Go away, old man'.

SMALL CHANGE. For heaven's sake, Sundari, please don't say that. The door is shut. We are alone together. What will the big boss think? I fall at your feet. I'll lose my job! Please!

OUTSIDE. Open the door! Quickly!

SMALL CHANGE. What on earth shall I do? How can I escape?

SAMBA. You said you didn't care!

SMALL CHANGE. I beg you, Sundari. I'll get you the job tomorrow. Please help me get away.

SAMBA. What can I do? There is no door to the toilet . . . I suggest you put on this sari and sit at the entrance. If the big boss asks, I shall say you came with me. Everything will be all right after he leaves. What do you say?

SMALL CHANGE. Wear a sari?

OUTSIDE. Who is that? What's happening inside?

SMALL CHANGE. Give it to me, quick! (*He puts on the sari in a great hurry.*)

Samba takes away his clothes and puts them where he cannot find them.

SAMBA. Who is that? Can't you wait till I come?

Shows him the place to sit and then opens the door. White Elephant and Shiva are outside.

I was changing inside. Such a racket out there! What's the hurry?

WHITE ELEPHANT. Who is this?

SHIVA. I don't know, sir. She said she was an acquaintance of yours.

WHITE ELEPHANT. Mine? Are you out of your mind? Where is that scoundrel Small Change? Grazing a donkey?

SHIVA. I don't know, sir.

WHITE ELEPHANT. Who are you?

SAMBA. Small Change said he would get me the P.A.'s job in White Elephant's office. I'm waiting for him.

WHITE ELEPHANT. The rogue! What was the King's order and what is this fellow doing here? I'll teach him a lesson. Look here, a guest of the King will be arriving soon. Will you please vacate the room?

SAMBA. The Chamberlain told me I could stay here because nobody else is expected.

WHITE ELEPHANT. Did the Chamberlain say that? That means no one else is coming. Why did you come here, Shiva? Aren't you looking after Ding Dong saheb?

SHIVA. You were banging on the door. I came to help you.

WHITE ELEPHANT. I don't need help from any one. Go away. Big deal! Comes like a god to help. (*To Samba*) Listen, you are an educated woman. You shouldn't let yourself be cheated by such useless loafers. He must be a real crook to have deceived you like this. Who knows how many more he has cheated in the same way. I shall take you to the King. You must tell him all about it.

SAMBA. Why only the King? I can tell it to his grandmother, too.

WHITE ELEPHANT. He had to send his sister to the King to get a job for himself. How does he imagine he can find a job for you?

SAMBA. He says he couldn't care less for you.

WHITE ELEPHANT. Damn him!

SAMBA. What is his name?

WHITE ELEPHANT. Loafer.

SAMBA. What's yours?

WHITE ELEPHANT. Donkey's Tail.

SAMBA. Please tell the King and get me a job, sir.

WHITE ELEPHANT. You don't need the King when I'm around. I'm not one to blow my own trumpet. But this I have to say—the kingdom exists because I exist. Do you know what would happen to this kingdom if I was absent even for a day?

SAMBA. What, sir?

WHITE ELEPHANT. It'd go bankrupt. Let the King hold court without me! I'd like to see if even one person in the court can write the King's name without a spelling mistake! Impossible! Running an office is not child's play. The King—the King of Spades—King Kalmadi—trembles at the sight of me. I have said all this to assure you of one thing. There is a job and you'll get it. But you must give me what you were about to give Small Change.

SAMBA. I trust you completely. Throw me in water, throw me in milk . . .

WHITE ELEPHANT. I will throw you in alcohol. Wait.

Shuts the door and comes over to Samba. Meanwhile the King and Chamberlain arrive outside.

SAMBA. I will die of anger!
How can I refrain
from consoling
this lady love
with her killing charms?

KING (*outside*). Have all the arrangements been made?

CHAMBERLAIN. Don't you worry, my lord. White Elephant has seen to everything.

White Elephant, drinking inside, becomes scared at hearing the King's voice. The King preens himself over and over again.

WHITE ELEPHANT. I think the King is outside.

SAMBA. Yes. It sounded like his voice.

KING. Has she come?

CHAMBERLAIN. She has indeed.

KING. You may go.

CHAMBERLAIN. As you wish, my lord.

KING. Take all the menials around here away with you when you go.

CHAMBERLAIN. Certainly, my lord.

WHITE ELEPHANT. Oh, I'm lost. Oh god, save me. Sundari, help me escape somehow! Please.

SAMBA. That is the only door to this room. Shall I open it?

WHITE ELEPHANT. No, no, no.

SAMBA. Why? Isn't the King afraid of you?

WHITE ELEPHANT. You don't understand, Sundari. I shall tell you everything later. But now please help me escape. I shall never forget your kindness.

KING (*lifts his arm and points to his armpit*). Are you leaving? Wait! See if I smell sweet. (*Chamberlain smells him. King lifts his other arm, pointing to the armpit.*)

CHAMBERLAIN. You need not lift anything else, my lord. All your limbs are fragrant.

KING. Call her. 'Sundari, the King is here. Open the door.' No, no. Say 'Sundari, His Highness is here. Open the door.' No, no. Say 'O great beauty, the handsomest man on earth, Maharaja Kalmadi is here.

Open the door and welcome him.' Or shall I sing a song asking the lady to open all doors?

CHAMBERLAIN. No, my lord. Why make a noise outside? You can sing inside if you wish.

KING. Yes. That's better. Then say 'The King has come. Open the door.' Or 'He is here. The door'. Or just say 'The door'. Or why say anything at all? Just knock on the door. That should be enough.

Chamberlain knocks on the door.

WHITE ELEPHANT. I beseech you, Sundari. Please save me somehow.

SAMBA. How? Look. You put on this sari and go in there. If I'm asked, I shall say that you came with me. Once the King leaves, there will be no problem. What do you say?

WHITE ELEPHANT. What? Wear a sari?

CHAMBERLAIN. Sundari, the King has come. Open the door, Sundari.

WHITE ELEPHANT. Give it here. I'll wear it.

CHAMBERLAIN. Sundari! Why aren't you opening the door?

SAMBA. Chamberlain, I've been waiting for the King all alone, and now I'm overcome with pangs of longing, lying on the bed. Was it right of your King to come so late? (*To White Elephant*) Wrap yourself up quick, you bastard, and go sit in the bog with your mouth and your arse shut. There's a woman in there. Take care not to finger her—I'm warning you.

He opens the door. The King comes in. Samba has covered his face with his sari.

KING. Oh my beloved! Ever since I was thrilled by the sight of you during the Spring Festival, my heart has gone blind, my life is barren, my body has withered, my mind is empty, my stomach is a pitcher. Why don't you come quickly and soothe the pain of my longing?

SAMBA. Your Highness, Sundari is hiding inside. She is terribly shy.

KING. Who are you?

SAMBA. I am her maid, my lord. Two sisters have come to serve you. The elder is called Manjari and the younger is Sundari. To start with, they are both good dancers. They are hoping you'll make up your mind to watch them dance.

KING. Oh no! I thought we two were alone. All right, let's first accept the homage of their art. Let them come.

SAMBA. Ladies, His Highness has agreed to accept your services. Come quickly and dance for him. (*They look at each other, very worried*) Can't you come out quickly? My lord is a true connoisseur. Do you desire him to come to where you are and drink from your lips? Come, come! My lord, they desire you to call them yourself. Will you satisfy their desire?

KING. Certainly. My beauties! Come here and show your art!

SAMBA. Don't be afraid, ladies. The King is a great lover of art. Come out quickly. Will you come at once or do you want the King to come in there? My lord! (*They both come out, scared*) There they come! I'll sing and they'll dance, my lord.

Oh King!
What fun!
Youth has blossomed anew!
Burning desire,
unquenchable thirst—
I call you, King, come, come!
I'm a juicy fruit,

a lovely woman lost to her body.
Why do you stare so?
Eat up and be happy!
Mind and body have blossomed—
come and ransack
my sprouting youth!
I waited for you in secret—
Why did you not come?
I cannot stand love's torture,
I won't take any argument.
Singing and running,
springing and swerving,
come laughing!

They both dance, out of time with the tune.

SAMBA. Your Highness, from now on there will be just you and your sweethearts. I shall take leave of you. My lord, my girls are still young and haven't been serviced. They may give some trouble. Please bear with them. You are a man of experience.

KING. Yes, indeed. And you too. Bolt the door from outside. Whatever happens, no one should be hovering around here till morning.

Samba takes the clothes of White Elephant and Small Change, runs out and closes the door.

SCENE NINE

Ganesha temple, Samba is laughing, Shiva seems depressed.

SHIVA. I said stop laughing!

SAMBA. Ha, ha, ha!

SHIVA. Have you gone mad?

SAMBA. By the grace of Ganesha, I haven't gone mad yet. Pray for our girl that she doesn't go mad.

SHIVA. Or perhaps we have gone mad.

SAMBA. Quite likely. They might think so. Shiva, do you think there might be some special liquor in the water of this city? I tell you, I've had many kinds of drinks in my life. But this sort of thing has never happened to me before. When I've had a little too much, the whole world seems upside down. I see two of everything. Little things look big and big things look small. Once, and only once, your mother looked like a cow. But no drink has ever before made everyone else appear insane. There must be some divine liquor in the water here.

SHIVA. You never think of anything else but liquor.

SAMBA. Think, my son! Have you ever seen or heard of a donkey finding its own bride—in stories or even in your dreams? When we want a bride, they won't even show their daughters to us, let alone give them in marriage. But they fall over one another in their eagerness to give them to that son of a donkey. You didn't see them, but two girls were standing there crying. I thought they were upset because they had been dragged out to get married to a donkey. I was glad I had discovered two human beings at last. But Shiva, do you know why they were crying? Your donkey had not chosen them. That's why. Women here deserve only donkeys. Ho! ho! ho!

SHIVA. I couldn't bear to look at the King. His face was scratched all over and his arms and legs were bandaged. Who knows what White Elephant and Small Change had done to him! Anyway, why are they not to be seen anywhere?

SAMBA. The same thing might have happened to them. Wounded all over . . .

SHIVA. While the bride was being chosen, the Chamberlain just wouldn't leave me in peace. He kept on whispering in my ear—Do you know Sundari? What has happened to her? I couldn't even get up and go away because Gajanimbe's turn hadn't come yet. Finally, she came, but the donkey just couldn't bray. She had almost gone away again, when I twisted the donkey's tail and it brayed. 'This is Ding Dong's choice, Your Highness!' I said and turned to look at him. The King was already wild with the Chamberlain . . .

SAMBA. What did he say?

SHIVA. He was saying, 'This is her, you bastard! The one with the green sari and blue blouse. You brought me some wretch and got my arms and legs broken.'

SAMBA. Oh ho! So it was Gajanimbe the King saw that day. Serves him right, the rascal!

SHIVA. Let him go to hell, but what will happen to me?

SAMBA. What's wrong with you? Everything is going your way. Gajanimbe is Ding Dong's wife. The wedding night is tonight. Go to Gajanimbe, tie up the donkey and enjoy yourself. Kick the donkey if it brays. That's all.

SHIVA. It's not all that easy. Do you know what the Chamberlain was plotting with the King?

SAMBA. What?

SHIVA. 'If this is the girl with the green sari and the blue blouse, we've caught her. Ding Dong has chosen her anyway. Let's arrange the wedding night tonight. As soon as the donkey enters the room, she'll start singing "Ay, ay, I can't live with a donkey. Help me, help me!" You can go in like a god and save her'. That's what he was saying. If I get caught, that'll be the end of me. What do we do now? Tell me.

SAMBA. What else? You go to Gajanimbe as we planned.

SHIVA. Nothing will be solved by you wearing a sari again. You wouldn't come out of it alive another time. You have to think about solving this problem now.

SAMBA. My only problem at the moment is your empty head. Shiva, you have Ganesha's blessings. Talk less and sharpen your wits. Work for it. If a donkey's dung and piss can fetch a thousand rupees, just calculate how much its braying will be worth.

SHIVA. What do you mean?

SAMBA. You stay with your donkey in Gajanimbe's room. Close the doors and windows tight. Don't open them whatever happens. If the King and the Chamberlain come, I'll whistle. Then you must make Ding Dong bray fiercely. That's all. I'll see to the rest. Go now.

SHIVA. Do you mean I should go?

SAMBA. Don't rub it in. Get lost!

Shiva goes off.

SCENE TEN

A song is heard from a distance. Moonlight. Ding Dong's wedding night. The King and the Chamberlain arrive, presuming the couple are busy inside. They are in disguise: the King is a male ghost, the Chamberlain a she-devil. Singing from a distance.

I can't live without you,
I can't forget you-u-u.
Pleasing one, playful one,
You who've won my heart,
I shall be hurt, O, love god!
I can't forget you.
The love god's flowered dart pierces my heart.
Alas! What can I do?
Handsome one, don't forget a maiden's pangs.
I throw myself on your mercy.
The bed of flowers burns with summer's heat.
I shall be hurt, O, love god!
I can't forget you.

KING. Are you sure no one will recognize us?

CHAMBERLAIN. Impossible, my lord. Especially you—you look exactly like a male ghost.

KING. You look like a she-devil too. I don't hear her moan.

CHAMBERLAIN. Maybe they aren't in bed. The light is still on.

KING. It's getting late. See if you can peep in from somewhere. Let's see what they're doing.

CHAMBERLAIN. And if somebody sees us watching?

KING. Who can see without my permission?

CHAMBERLAIN. Don't make such a noise, my lord.

KING. I can make as much noise as I want. Who are you to question me?

CHAMBERLAIN. My lord, my lord, the whole town has its ears in this direction today. If we get caught peeping, they will look at us with contempt.

KING. Say so then. Think of a plan which will make them look at us with respect.

CHAMBERLAIN. What for?

KING. See if there's a hole in the door to peep through.

CHAMBERLAIN. No, my lord.

KING. See if there's a chink in the window.

CHAMBERLAIN. No, my lord.

KING. All right. Put your ears to the wall and see if you can hear them talking.

CHAMBERLAIN. I can't hear them, my lord.

KING. No hole, no chink, and you can't hear them talking! You bastard! Why did you arrange the wedding night in such a place? Climb upon the roof and remove a tile. Look down and tell me what they're doing.

Chamberlain climbs up and starts giving a false report.

CHAMBERLAIN. My lord, they are sitting on the bed.

KING. I see. And then?

CHAMBERLAIN. Ding Dong is whispering something in her ear.

KING. Quickly! What else? She's laughing. Laughing? Is she laughing for joy or for sadness?

CHAMBERLAIN. For joy, my lord.

KING (*pulls him by the legs and makes him fall*). You bastard! This is the girl I was talking about from the beginning. You brought me someone else and put me to no end of trouble. Why should she sing for help when she's laughing happily? How can I save her if she doesn't sing out? You son of a bitch! Do one thing at least. You have removed a tile anyway. Put your face through the gap and hoot like an owl. Maybe she'll get scared and come out.

Chamberlain obeys. Just then Samba's whistle is heard. Ding Dong brays heroically. Both run away scared—they run some distance. Samba is sitting there, wrapped in a blanket and drinking.

KING. Do you think Ding Dong recognized us?

CHAMBERLAIN. That's impossible, my lord.

Samba slowly removes the blanket from his face.

SAMBA. You sons of thieves! Come over here.

CHAMBERLAIN. He's a drunkard.

KING. We'll say we're spirits. He'll run away scared. I shall sing a song about despair. Let's both sit and cry.

SAMBA. Come here! Stealing when you should be making love! Rascals! Even ghostly ghosts and devils make love at this hour. You, being human . . .

KING. We are ghosts and devils too.

SAMBA. Which one of you is the ghost and which the devil?

KING. This is the ghost.

CHAMBERLAIN. And this is the devil.

SAMBA. You are perfectly matched! Why are you wandering around instead of making love?

KING. We were, but we heard your voice.

SAMBA. Say so. Everyone is happy in this world. My son and daughter-in-law, the King and his Chamberlain, that Ding Dong and his she-ass, all the husbands and wives of this town, you and your devil—everyone is happy. It's only me, poor lonesome me, who's so unhappy (*Weeps loudly*.)

KING (*crying*). I feel like crying too, at your sadness.

SAMBA. Don't cry. I can't bear it. If someone else cries, whether they're human or ghosts and devils, I just can't bear it. Here, here's a drink. It'll do your soul good. (*The King gulps it down*) See, brother, we've drunk from the same pot. We are like brothers now, aren't we?

KING. Of course.

SAMBA. What were you doing before I came? Making love? Why should you stop because of me? Go ahead, make love! I shall watch you and feel happy. Go on!

KING. No, brother. She feels shy.

SAMBA. You can't let her be because she's shy. You shouldn't give women so much freedom. You should keep kicking her around. What kind of customs do you have in your world, anyway?

KING. What customs?

SAMBA. For instance, you are my brother, but you are a ghost. If I had an affair with your wife, what would you do to her? Throw her out of your community?

CHAMBERLAIN (*laughing*). You die and come off with us to our world. You can stay with us.

SAMBA. Brother ghost! You have a clever wife and she's very pretty too. (*Chamberlain laughs even more*) I have many friends who are ghosts. Do you know, even now when I go to my village, a she-devil comes at nights, gives me a jug of liquor and sleeps with me.

KING. You are very fortunate.

SAMBA. I don't touch her if she doesn't bring me liquor.

CHAMBERLAIN. Good for you!

SAMBA. She's no ordinary devil. You know, the king of the ghosts—his daughter. A princess devil!

KING. Really?

SAMBA. Who do you think I am? Do you think I'd fall for any shameless devil ready to open her legs? Do you know how I got her?

KING. Tell me.

SAMBA. It was a dark moonless night like this. I was as drunk as I am now. My human wife had died just two days before. I went to the graveyard to see how she was getting on. Thousands of ghosts and devils were there, holding court. The king was sitting on the throne, and beside him the queen devil. Next to her a beautiful young devil, sparkling. She's the one that became my mistress later. My wife hadn't come to life there yet. Her name hadn't been entered in the attendance register. The court was being held in grand style. All sorts of ghosts and devils were performing gymnastics before the king. Everyone was laughing and clapping. I got into the spirit of it. I went up to the king, and jumped and did a cartwheel, like this. There was clapping and whistling all round. The king was so impressed that he gave me the young princess. The ghost king looked exactly like you. I can do a cartwheel here like I did there. Will you be generous like the other king?

KING. Certainly. Most certainly. But first tell me about the princess. Does she come to you still?

SAMBA. Of course.

KING. Then why isn't she here?

SAMBA. Well, she lives in my village. I asked her to come with me. Do you know what she said? She said, 'Oh my darling! We are country bumpkins. The city devils will laugh at us. You go alone.'

CHAMBERLAIN. Then you are suffering miserably here, all alone.

SAMBA. That's true. I told her, 'Darling, I shall be cold without you. What shall I do?' Do you know what she did? She gave me a pearl and said, 'Beloved, when you feel very cold, put this pearl in someone's mouth and he'll turn into a woman.'

KING (*getting up excitedly*). Do you have the pearl with you now?

SAMBA. Yes, I do.

KING. Give it here.

SAMBA. I don't want you. I don't like your beard. Shall we give it to this woman?

KING. Go ahead.

CHAMBERLAIN (*scared*). Your Highness, must I take it? Must I?

KING. Yes. At once.

CHAMBERLAIN. My lord, I suspect something. I don't want it.

KING. I said take it.

SAMBA. Put it in your mouth! (*He gives it to him. Samba is happy. The King is curious.*)

CHAMBERLAIN (*putting the pearl in his mouth*). Oh my god! Your Highness, look! I really have become a woman. Please, please make me a man again!

KING. Really?

CHAMBERLAIN. How can I tell you, my lord? I am really a woman now.

KING. It has happened for the best. Let Gajanimbe sleep with the donkey. You come with me. (*He goes up to her*.)

Samba comes in the way.

SAMBA. Hey, you bastard, watch out! I'm the one who made him into a woman. I want her. Who do you think you are? (*Takes hold of Chamberlain's hand*) Let her stay here until I warm up. I'll send her back later.

KING. Son of a bitch, who do *you* think I am? I am the King of this country.

SAMBA. You lying scoundrel. You are a nameless ghost. How dare you say you are the King? Look at your face. If you touch her, I'll kick you. Go away or else . . .

Goes up and hits him. The King staggers and falls. When Samba tries to hit him again, he runs. When the Chamberlain tries to run after him, calling out 'My lord', Samba pulls her back.

Lie down without any fuss. If you make a noise, I won't leave you in peace till morning. Watch out!

SCENE ELEVEN

Palace. King, sitting. Chamberlain, now a woman, holding her sari over her face.

CHAMBERLAIN. Your Highness!

KING. Who are you?

CHAMBERLAIN. I am your Chamberlain, my lord.

KING. Oh yes, so you are! Come. Haven't you taken off your sari yet?

CHAMBERLAIN. It would be pointless, my lord. I'm still a woman.

KING. Really?

CHAMBERLAIN. Why should I lie, my lord? I'm truly a woman now.

KING. Is that so? You look very pretty.

CHAMBERLAIN. It's a joke to you, my lord. How can I show my face to others in this shape? Please, somehow, make me a man again.

KING. Why didn't you ask him that?

CHAMBERLAIN. I begged and beseeched him, my lord, to change me back into a man. He just growled at me and told me to keep quiet because I look better like this.

KING. What he said is true, my man . . . no, my woman.

CHAMBERLAIN. We can accommodate him when he's cold, but how can I be a woman all the time? He won't say no to you. Please send for him and tell him, Your Highness.

KING. It's difficult. I don't know who that rascal is or where he stays. In fact I don't know anything about him. How can I send for him?

CHAMBERLAIN. I believe he stays in the Ganesha temple. He asked me to go there today.

KING. Very well, then. Wait here. By the way, Chamberlain, how does Ding Dong approach his wife?

CHAMBERLAIN. What do you mean?

KING. Imagine it's night. People eat and sleep at night. Let's imagine we've eaten. Now it's time to sleep. You are Gajanimbe. You are lying on the bed over there. Ding Dong is in the stable next door. A man and wife should, of course, sleep together.

CHAMBERLAIN. Of course.

KING. How?

CHAMBERLAIN. I haven't seen them, my lord. Samba says he has seen them.

KING. Is that so? How does he go to her?

CHAMBERLAIN. He bathes before eating his supper. After his supper, he eats betel leaves and sprays perfume all over his body. His foreleg is decorated with jasmine. Then he brays, comes out and dances a jig before Gajanimbe's door. Gajanimbe opens the door and says, 'O my king, give me joy.' He dances in happily.

KING. Splendid! He's quite a voluptuary, that Ding Dong bastard, in spite of being a donkey. What does Shiva do in the meanwhile?

CHAMBERLAIN. He sings a love song.

KING. Chamberlain, the man we met must be a great magician. He can turn a man into a woman. He moves freely with ghosts and devils . . .

CHAMBERLAIN. Yes my lord. He is a great magician, as you say.

KING. Listen, Chamberlain, if he can turn you into a woman, maybe he can turn me into a donkey.

CHAMBERLAIN. Maybe he can. But I don't see why you want to become a donkey.

KING. Imbecile! First go and bring Ding Dong.

CHAMBERLAIN. My lord . . .

KING. I'll tell you later—you go and bring him first.

SCENE TWELVE

Shiva and Gajanimbe.

SHIVA. Listen to me.

GAJANIMBE. No. I won't.

SHIVA. Who do you think you're speaking to? I'm your husband.

GAJANIMBE. According to the law, a donkey is my husband, not you.

SHIVA. Who am I then?

GAJANIMBE. Shiva.

SHIVA. Then I won't say anything.

GAJANIMBE. Why not? Please keep saying something.

SHIVA. Why should I say something to someone who doesn't like it?

GAJANIMBE. If you speak I'll start liking it.

SHIVA. All right, then, go inside, shut the door tight and sit down.

GAJANIMBE. What will happen if I go on sitting outside here?

SHIVA. There is going to be a commotion. It'll be all men and a woman has no place in it.

GAJANIMBE. It'll add to the colour if women are around. (*Just then someone comes running in and hides*) I am getting scared.

SHIVA. Why didn't you go to your parents'?

GAJANIMBE. If I go there, the neighbours' children dance and sing, 'There comes the donkey's wife!'

SHIVA. Go in quietly now and shut the door. Don't open it till you hear my voice.

Gajanimbe goes inside. The police enter.

POLICE. Did the ex-Minister come this way?

SHIVA. No.

Police go away. After making sure they have gone, the person in hiding comes out.

MINISTER. You have done me a great favour.

SHIVA. It's dangerous for you to be here, sir.

MINISTER. I know that.

SHIVA. Are you the ex-Minister?

MINISTER. If I was, would you feel sorry you'd saved me?

SHIVA. Certainly not.

MINISTER. Yes. I am the ex-Minister.

SHIVA. You shouldn't expose yourself to such danger. Why did you come here, sir?

MINISTER. I came to see you, my man.

SHIVA. Tell me, sir. What can I do?

MINISTER. Our revolution has fizzled out. There is no deliverance from this monster. It's not your donkey I'm angry at. It's fitting that he should be the Minister. Who else could be, with a king like this? But how he has taxed the people in the name of that poor, dumb animal! The demon! How can people live?

SHIVA. Like king, like subjects. Isn't that so, sir?

MINISTER. That's true too. Never mind, let's leave it at that. There are not as many revolutionaries as before. Some are in jail and some are in heaven. A couple of us are still alive. Today or tomorrow, we shall be finished off too. It will be better so. I feel ashamed to be alive after losing all my companions. I want to ask a small favour of you, my man.

SHIVA. What can I do?

MINISTER. I have a friend who's a washerman. He has a family, but he's now a pauper because he got involved in the revolution. Help him if you can.

SHIVA. What can I do?

MINISTER. He has a she-donkey, called Radha. It's plump and healthy. I believe your Ding Dong needs a new mate every day. Use his animal and give him a good price. Poor fellow. He'll survive somehow.

SHIVA. Come this way, sir. Someone's coming.

Minister hides, Samba comes running in.

SAMBA. I've been searching for you for ages, son.

SHIVA. Why, Father?

SAMBA. I must tell you something in secret. Is there anyone around?

SHIVA. No. Tell me.

SAMBA. The King is up to something today. (*Shiva points towards the hiding man and gestures that he should whisper*) What I want to say is . . . (*whispers in Shiva's ear*).

SHIVA. What for? (*Samba whispers.*)

SHIVA. When? (*Samba whispers.*)

SHIVA. What time? (*Samba whispers.*)

SHIVA. Oh, I see. So this is what it has come to . . . Sir, come out. Tell your friend to bring Radha here tonight. If possible, be here with the remaining revolutionaries.

MINISTER. There are no revolutionaries left. Even the few that survived have stopped seeing me because they don't understand my position.

SAMBA. Sir, did you have a follower called Birayya?

MINISTER. He's a lazy fellow.

SAMBA. Tell him that the dam has to be broken, and he should bring the pick and crowbar. He'll come.

MINISTER. What do you mean by dam?

SAMBA. Just tell him that, sir.

MINISTER. All right.

SCENE THIRTEEN

The King, Chamberlain as a woman and Samba come on from one side of the stage. The King is already half dressed up. Everything possible is being done to make him look like a donkey. He has a tail. They have come here to finish the job.

KING. Have you sent the army away from here?

CHAMBERLAIN. Yes, I have.

KING. Ding Dong?

CHAMBERLAIN. I untied him and chased him out of town.

KING. The guards?

CHAMBERLAIN. I have sent them elsewhere. No one's around, Your Highness. There's no one to answer even if Gajanimbe does scream with fright.

KING. Fright? Why? Don't I look like Ding Dong?

SAMBA. Yes. You must finish dressing. Then you'll look like the grandfather of all Ding Dongs.

KING. I don't want to look like his grandfather. Just make me look like Ding Dong.

SAMBA. Come here, then.

They take off his clothes piece by piece and dress him up as a donkey.

KING. Comb my tail a bit. (*They comb it*) Comb my mane. (*They obey*) Mirror! (*They give it to him, he looks in it*) Perfume! (*They spray it on him.*)

SAMBA. Whatever we do your kingly dignity shows through, my lord. You are a royal donkey.

KING (*joyfully*). What will Gajanimbe think?

SAMBA. She'll love you more than ever today.

CHAMBERLAIN. My lord, this is Gajanimbe's bedroom.

SAMBA. The light is still on. She is waiting for you, Your Highness.

KING. Don't call me 'Your Highness'. Call me Ding Dong. Check if everything is all right?

SAMBA. Admirable!

KING. You go over there and start singing. Shall I bray? Hee-haw, hee-haw . . . Wait, wait! My finger is showing.

SAMBA. If you go down on your hands, it'll be hidden in the grass, my lord.

KING. Yes, of course. Do I graze now?

SAMBA. Not now. Later. Start dancing.

KING. Hee-haw-haw-haw . . . u-hu-hu-haw-haw . . . How was it?

CHAMBERLAIN. Aah! My hair stood on end.

SAMBA. What did you say? I'm feeling cold.

KING. How was my braying?

SAMBA. Not so good. Raise your voice.

KING. Hee-haw-haw-haw, hee-haw-haw-haw . . .

SAMBA. You must straighten up. Let's see you dance a little. (*King dances*) You should bray and dance at the same time. (*King does so*) Ah ha! That's how Ding Dong looks. Hey, *you* sing . . .

CHAMBERLAIN (*sings*). It's cold,
it's cold,
I cannot bear this cold, hee-haw!

SHIVA (*from the other side*). Oh, the play has begun. Where's the washerman?

KING. Hee-haw-haw-haw, hee-haw-haw-haw (*Comes forward, braying.*)

Shiva pretends to be looking for Ding Dong.

SHIVA. Who is it? Is it His Royal Highness Ding Dong saheb? (*The King is silent*) Maybe not. If it was, he would bray with love immediately.

KING. Hee-haw-haw-haw, hee-haw-haw-haw . . .

SHIVA. If it was, he would stiffen his tail and shake himself as soon as he saw me. (*King does so*) Where is the fragrant smell of his perfume? (*King lifts his arms and displays his armpits*) Why isn't he dancing with joy today? (*King dances*) This is indeed our Ding Dong saheb. No doubt about it. I am your humble servant Shivanna, sir.

KING. Hee-haw, hee-haw, hee-haw . . .

SHIVA. Sir, I have to tell you that it is not right for you to escape from me and disappear from the stable. (*King hangs his head as if to say he is sorry*) I looked for you everywhere in town, sir. Here are your favourite onions and chillies. Please eat them. (*King looks at Shiva, scared*) What is this? You always eat them to give you strength to make love. Sir, why aren't you eating today? Or perhaps this is not our Ding Dong saheb? (*King eats anxiously and is in agony*) That's my master, all right. How were the chillies and onions, sir?

KING. Hee-haw, hee-haw, hee-haw . . .

SHIVA. You should be lying down with your darling wife by now, sir.

KING (*nods vigorously*). Hee-haw, hee-haw.

SHIVA. Why isn't my great master sleepy? Oh, I know. Your servant knows all your secrets, sir. Don't worry. I won't tell your queen. You escaped into town because of the washerman's donkey Radha, didn't you?

KING (*as if to say yes*). Hee-haw, hee-haw.

SHIVA. Is she so beautiful, sir?

KING (*shyly*). Hee-haw.

SHIVA. Radha came here looking for you while you were there.

KING (*shyly*). Hee, hee, hee.

SHIVA. Isn't your humble servant here to fulfil your desires? Now, let's see you bray 'Radha' once.

KING. Hee-haw-haw-haw-haw!

Radha brays from the other side. While the King is looking at Shiva, astonished, people bring Radha in with ropes and machetes in their hands.

SHIVA. They have brought Radha for you, sir.

The King tries to run away. Birayya puts a rope around the King's neck and holds on to him.

Don't run away like that, sir. Radha is suffering because she is parted from you. Have you brought your ropes and machetes?

BIRAYYA. Yes, we have.

SHIVA. Look, when Ding Dong saheb starts to climb on her, Radha must not lower her tail, nor should she shout with pain, nor bray. If she does any of those things, you will lose one third of the fee. Is that understood?

WASHERMAN. Yes, sir.

SHIVA. After climbing on, our saheb will concentrate his mind and rest his chin for some time. During that time, your Radha must not move here and there or back and forth. If she moves, you will lose another third of the fee.

BIRAYYA. All right, sir. That's why we've brought sticks, ropes, whips, clubs and so on.

SHIVA. In the meantime, our saheb will give Radha ten different varieties of kisses or bites. He may poke her in various places with his hooves. Your Radha must comply at all times, otherwise you will lose the rest of the fee.

BIRAYYA. If she acts up I'll beat her to a pulp. Look, I've brought a machete too.

SHIVA. Are you sure Radha has no gonorrhoea or other diseases?

WASHERMAN. No, sir. I have a doctor's certificate.

SHIVA (*to the King*). My duty is done, sir. It's your turn now.

In the meanwhile, the King has been trying to run away, but they have not let him. The donkey is already tied up. Everyone is standing around shouting and egging them on. They push and beat the King cruelly every time he gets away. This goes on for a long time and the King's clothes are in shreds. In the madness of victory, they torture him even more.

WASHERMAN. Did you think it was a new tax, rascal?

KING. Please don't. I am your King. Save me!

BIRAYYA. Look at the cheek of this donkey. Calls itself the King. You ass! You want to insult our King, do you?

Birayya beats him. King escapes and runs. Everyone chases him. At this juncture, everyone present is chasing the King and shouting 'Catch him, catch him'. The King now stands at the far end of the stage.

KING. Let me go! Aren't I your King? As his subjects are, so the king will be. If you are worthless, how can I be any better? I shall run away from this country. Let me go! I shall never come back. Please let me live!

The people throw more stones at him. King runs away.

MINISTER. Thank heavens! We have got rid of the pest.

WASHERMAN. Victory to the revolutionary Minister!

MINISTER. The victory is for everyone. Samba and Shiva are the architects of our victory. You must thank them.

SHIVA. Who will be the King now? Whoever it is, I have one request to make.

MINISTER. No more kings! We will have elections and rule ourselves. Since we are all here, you may tell us your request.

SHIVA. It's just this. Although Gajanimbe was married to the donkey, I was the one who was living with her. Please free her from the donkey and let her be married to me.

MINISTER. Most certainly (*He joins their hands together.*)

Clapping all round. Ganesha enters.

GANESHA. I've been looking for you high and low.

SHIVA. Why, god?

GANESHA. Where is your father?

Samba comes and folds his hands.

SAMBA. I'm blessed by the sight of your feet, lord.

GANESHA. Never mind. Where is that pearl. Give it to me.

SAMBA. Which pearl, god?

GANESHA. Come on now! You know which pearl. The one which turns men into women when they put it in their mouths.

SAMBA. Must I give it back, god?

GANESHA. Hey! It's not mine. It's my father's. Do you know what my father said when I didn't return it?

SAMBA. What did he say, god?

GANESHA. Son, I don't know what you are doing with that pearl, but it must be the reason why you have so few devotees. See how he has misjudged me!

SAMBA. In that case I'll give it back to you at once. (*He drags over the Chamberlain*) Give me that pearl in your mouth!

CHAMBERLAIN. Oh, that? I haven't got it.

SAMBA. Just shut up and give it to me.

CHAMBERLAIN. I haven't got it. At first I used to take it out when you left me. But then I started living with you most of the time, so I swallowed it.

SAMBA. Oh, my god! What shall I tell Lord Ganesha?

SHIVA. Through your kindness, god, the whole country is happier, and I'm happier too.

SAMBA (*holding the Chamberlain's hand*). I am happier too, lord.

SHIVA. We shall all sing your praises. Forget the pearl and bless us so we may prosper.

GANESHA. All . . . right.

SAMBA. By the way, where is Ding Dong?

GANESHA. He came near the temple and I put him back into the picture.

SHIVA. Thank god! Come, let's all offer our prayers to Ganesha.

All line up at the front of the stage. The King comes in too, no longer dressed as a donkey.

SHIVA. You said you'd leave the country. Why have you come back?

KING. I'm an actor!

ALL (*folding their hands*). Sri Ganesha . . .

Curtain.

SIRI SAMPIGE

A Play in Sixteen Scenes

Translated from the Kannada by
Rowenna Hill
with K. P. Vasudevan and N. S. Ramaswamy

INTRODUCTION

Tradition is a much misunderstood word in India today. That it is a Western import (from the Latin *tradere*—to 'hand over' or 'deliver') is the last thing in the minds of those who believe themselves to be its votaries. What the urban Indian artist, desperately seeking his roots, is doing is not so much 'inheriting' tradition as 'inventing' it. Certainly, this is worlds removed from native notions of 'parampara' but let us clarify. In traditional art forms like music and dance, we are still in unbroken contact with the past. But in modern art forms like 'drama' (to use an older nomenclature), it is a truism that what we have is really the anglicized Parsi theatre from the close of the century. It is the tradition of this theatre that has inspired the popular or commercial stage with its various gimmicks such as the revolving stage, cyclorama and of late, even shameless borrowings from the cinema, much admired in plays, produced in Madras.

It is against this background of groping for roots that Chandrasekhar Kambar's ethnic theatre has to be placed and evaluated. I still retain vivid memories of the explosive impact of his *Jokumaraswami* in 1972 in the alfresco setting at the back of Ravindra Kalakshetra that B. V. Karanth had devised for it. Something still needs to be said of the bayalata form in which this early play was so imaginatively clothed. Bayalata, as Kambar is never tired of repeating, is *total theatre*. It includes 'dance, drama, narrative, song, sex, death and religion' (Kambar, 'Folk Theatre as I See It'; see pp. 257–61 in this volume.) Both the audience and the actors participate in 'what is ultimately a shared religious experience in the form of a play' (ibid.) A traditional bayalata performance begins with prayer and ends with the audience as well as the players going to a temple early in the morning. Certainly,

Jokumaraswami began with a prayer, but it ended with a call for the birth of a more just society. Of course, Kambar is aware that in times of change, bayalata—relevant only to organic, undivided societies—cannot survive. His subsequent experiments in theatre have taken him beyond bayalata. He has now turned to yakshagana and its possibilities for theatre today.

The revival of the yakshagana form owes a great deal to Shivram Karanth, although many feel that he has 'bourgeosified' the folk form and trimmed it to suit Western and Festival of India audiences. By etiolating the form and removing dialogue altogether, he has brought it closer to Western ballet and has, to quote theatre historian Rustom Bharucha, 'diluted rather than strengthened the energies of the "folk".' Marathi playwright Mahesh Elkunchwar has acidly characterized the borrowings of this theatre as 'artistic kleptomania'. Kambar has tampered far less with the native form; his chief innovation has been the introduction of the playwright with its modern connotations. This has entailed a shift from the third-person narrative of traditional yakshagana to a more dramatic form where the individual voices of the characters are allowed to be heard. The only restriction on the playwright is that he has to imaginatively enter into the world of the community's myths and deploy these myths to structure his plays.

Siri Sampige, the fruit of such a creative intervention into traditional practices (which is basically 'symbiotic' rather than 'parasitical', or so Kambar claims), was made possible through a Ford Foundation fellowship. The writing of the play began in May 1986, (the well-known yakshagana bhagawathar, Sri Prabhakar Hegde, was summoned to Bangalore to assist in the process) and by July 1986 the first draft was ready. The scene now shifts to Heggodu, a tiny village in Shimoga, where the play went into production under the direction of K. V. Subbanna, 'the modest visionary', who has been the guiding spirit of the cultural organization Ninasam. The play was extensively revised and rewritten several times and suggestions from B. V. Karanth (who was present) were incorporated. On 21 August 1986, the play was finally staged in Heggodu; and on 28 August the same year, it was produced in New Delhi at the Ford Foundation workshop at Sri Ram Centre for Arts and Culture.

The question remains: How much does Kambar's *Siri Sampige* go beyond a traditional yakshagana performance to justify his claim that it is a legitimate extension of a basically religious form (with its attendant notions of punya for those witnessing it) into the secular domain of the 'modern stage'? In other words, have we here moved from the *celebratory* mode of traditional yakshagana to the *critical* mode of modern playwriting? Does the absence of a shared myth between audience and playwright automatically and unfailingly activate the critical consciousness?

A brief glance at the plot of *Siri Sampige* might be in order here. The Prince of Shivapura, son of King Nagara Nayaka, has reached the age of sixteen when, by his mother's wish, he is to be married. But the Prince meanwhile has fallen in love with the impossibly perfect lamp maiden who comes to life one night in his bed chamber and disappears, dancing, into his own body. His account of this experience is couched in the most extraordinary terms and worth noting: while he was 'all alone and fast asleep . . . the wall of this palace cracked, and someone drew a sword from its scabbard and let my thighs feel its edge'. He now demands that his body be split in two, and the equal parts stuffed into two pots. Out of one he emerges unscathed (as he, according to prophecy, can only die if his brother dies and he happens to be the sole heir to the throne). But out of the other pot emerges not the lamp maiden of his dreams but a hooded cobra. Marriage to Siri Sampige, daughter of King Pushparaja of Sevantipura, ensues but the Prince, in the grip of his earlier infatuation, will have nothing to do with his young wife. He periodically takes to visiting the lamp maiden in a pool outside the town and into which he gazes. Meanwhile, Siri Sampige herself has been charmed by the snake god, Kalinga, yields to him and conceives. Suspecting his wife's infidelity, the Prince orders a trial in which Siri Sampige proves her chastity: she takes the snake, which coils round the nagalinga, onto her body but remains unharmed. In the end, in a fit of jealousy, the Prince kills the snake and dies himself, fulfilling the ancient prophecy that he will die upon the death of his brother.

The play, then, recapitulates the growth of human consciousness from simple narcissism to full adulthood and genital sexuality. The symbolism of the snake is unmistakable, not only from the abundant Freudian literature but also explicitly in the play itself, when Siri Sampige becomes pregnant by Kalinga who turns out to be the 'rejected body' of the Prince. In the parallel subplot, involving the court jesters, Awali and Jawali, the sexual theme reappears: Jawali can make love to Kamala only when he turns into a snake. The negative influence of the Prince's mother on his sexual development (which we may broadly characterize as his 'Oedipal' problems) cannot be ignored. Widowed when the Prince was barely a year old, the Queen Mother dotes on him and cripples him emotionally. The collective deaths of the Prince and Kalinga, as well as their thematic doubles, Awali and Jawali, may be viewed as the tragedy of the self-regarding narcissistic self. The play punctuates in wholly Indian, non-derivative terms the passage of maturity. In achieving these larger truths through the use of indigenous myths, *Siri Sampige* goes way beyond traditional yakshagana.

T. G. Vaidyanathan
1991

A NOTE ON YAKSHAGANA

This play is written in the form of yakshagana. Narration is the soul of this form and it makes extensive use of song, mime and dance to create a total theatrical experience. The Bhagavata (narrator) tells the story in the third person and other characters dramatize in the first person what he narrates. In the beginning, the characters have no independent existence; they are simply a passive part of the narrative. Later, they become full-blooded characters. While the Bhagavata is singing the story, the characters interpret it through mime and dance. Later, they transform the same song into a dramatic event.

Chandrasekhar Kambar
1991

Siri Sampige was first produced in Kannada by Ninasam at Shivaramakaranth Rangamandira in Heggodu on 21 August 1986 and then at New Delhi at the Sri Ram Centre for Art and Culture on 28 August 1986 with the following cast:

PRINCE 1	Gopal Heranjal
PRINCE 2	T. Narayana Bhatt
KALINGA	Madhav Nayak
AWALI	Chandrasekhar
JAWALI	Manjappa
QUEEN MOTHER	Sushila
SIRI SAMPIGE	Sudha
LAMP MAIDEN	Sarada
KAMALA	Phaniyamma
BHAGAVATA	Prabhakar Hegde
ELDERS	Yesu Prakash
	Iqbal Ahmad
	Ganapati
	Prabhakar
	Srinivas
DIRECTION	K. V. Subbanna and Atul Tiwari
DANCE	Madhav Nayak and
	Gopal Heranjal
COSTUME AND STAGE	C. R. Jambe

The Hindi version of this play was produced by Goa Kala Akademi Theatre Art Faculty on 9 May 1990 and directed by B. Jayasree.

SCENE 1

Bhagavata and the chorus.

BHAGAVATA (as *dedication*). Before we speak, a thousand salutations
to you, great Lord Shiva of Savalagi,
split in your divine play into man and wife,
dancing Nataraja Ardhanarishwara,
body and mind, spirit and matter you are,
split into two and beyond duality, hail Shiva!
On Earth, shining Shivapura's
King Nagara Raya is dead.
Queen Mayavati lives and rightfully rules.

The Queen Mother, Mayavati, enters.

QUEEN MOTHER. Hear me! I am Mayavati, rightful wife of King Nagara Nayaka of Shivapura, city whose virtue shines upon the earth. My revered husband, after a long and virtuous reign, was borne away by Time into timelessness. Since then, I, like my revered husband, have continued to look after the interests of my subjects without the slightest flaw in my attention to them. And now to tell you of my household affairs, in brief. When my revered husband departed this life, our son Shivanaga was only a year old. As well as looking after my subjects, I took constant care in loving and feeding him. I was happy watching his infant antics. From his fifth year onwards, my son received from the mouth of a teacher the knowledge of all weapons and scriptures. Growing day by day like the waxing moon, he has now reached the age of sixteen, heir not only to his father's kingdom and treasury but also to his courage, daring and other virtues. Strong as a mountain, he is well fitted to be the lord of forest and field in this kingdom. While I was looking forward to being relieved of my worries after his coronation, one day a strange incident occurred. Hear!

BHAGAVATA. Our family god spoke through an oracle, and
foretold his future. See! Two dangers threaten:
When his voice breaks, he may become a monk,
When his brother dies, he dies too.

QUEEN MOTHER. How should it be that, on a full-moon day, the milk to be offered to our family god was curdled, an inauspicious sign? While I was thinking with my head in my hands, 'Oh Shiva, why should this happen?' our family god spoke through an oracle in the palace to tell me why. What he said was this: 'Daughter, there are two hindrances in the way of your son's good fortune. When his voice breaks, he may become a monk. If not he may die because of one who is heir to what he is heir to.' On hearing his words, I anxiously grasped the feet of the god and said, 'Lord god, I will offer you the taste of palm wine, I will perform the five-torch ritual for you, I will build you a temple at Shiva's right hand and place offerings at your holy feet. Let my son's family be a family of milk and gold. Let him be without troubles, oh lord!' Our family god blessed me with a small smile and said, 'When your son's voice breaks, arrange without delay for his marriage. Make sure he does not see his own image in water. Beware!' Thus saying, he vanished. Since I have borne no other child, my son's life is not in danger. But if the Prince sees his own image in water or in a mirror, he may become disinterested in worldly pleasures and wealth, and his mind may turn towards the ascetic life. Thus I myself have looked after my son with care so that he should not see his own image in water. My son is of robust beauty and lively. He can neither stand still nor sit still, but like a fresh young bull is always active, and I have seen the young girls of the clan sighing as they watch him. Just a few days ago his voice broke, and now we cannot delay any longer. After his marriage has been celebrated, he is to be crowned. To this, the people have given their consent, but the Prince himself evades it each time with a new excuse. So many maidens have been shown to him, but he is always disappointed. I am worried now whether there exists anywhere on earth a maiden he can admire. The more he makes excuses and postpones the wedding, the more my worries and anxieties increase. The Prince has now to be called and forced into marriage. So be it. Listen, Bhagavata!

BHAGAVATA. Speak, lady!

QUEEN MOTHER. Send for the Prince immediately!

Enter the Prince.

PRINCE. Mother, I bow to your lotus feet. You sent word telling me to come immediately. For what reason, Mother?

QUEEN MOTHER. Son—

BHAGAVATA. The Mother said, 'My son, your voice
has broken, so this is the right
time to marry. Hear me now
wed a woman and rule the world,
please your mother and live long!'

QUEEN MOTHER. Child, you have to be informed of a very important matter; that is why you have been called. I am only a woman and becoming old, and I can no longer bear the responsibility of the kingdom, so I desire to celebrate your marriage in a way acceptable to you, witness your coronation and spend the rest of my life in peace. The Elders of the family have therefore been sent to Sevantipura to see King Pushparaja's daughter Siri Sampige, and have approved her as a bride for you. Now, you must accept.

PRINCE. Why do you want me to marry straightaway, tying a grinding stone round the neck of a child at play? Why should responsibility fall on me while there are the Elders living? Please don't make me unhappy, Mother, by constantly telling me such cruel things.

QUEEN MOTHER. Do not foster our anxieties, dear son, by continuing to say no. Our lineage has been hurt with curses and sighs. You were raised with care and cunning, in order not to offend the pride of the family god or allow the eyes of the evil gods to fall on you. If some whirlwind sweeps away the plant raised by our sweat, then what will be the future of the lineage, my dear? Enough of the obstinacy you have shown lately! You don't want your mother's worries about your marriage to burn her to death with their pain, do you?

PRINCE. Kindly do not speak such words, Mother! If you feel pain in your mind, please forgive me. Only because the maidens you chose all had some defect or other, I have refused to marry. For no other reason.

QUEEN MOTHER. Which maiden is flawless? Son, if you want such a maiden, then you yourself must be your own wife.

PRINCE. I have faith that a flawless one must exist, Mother. From the day my voice broke, I have felt that she is hiding somewhere, like butter in milk. She is trying to come out of her hiding place. Give me time to show her to you.

QUEEN MOTHER. Do you need time to tell me the name of the maiden you admire? Or is this just another excuse to postpone the marriage? That's enough. You shall have one week's time to say who the maiden is. If you give me her name, well and good. If not, you will marry Siri Sampige. Is that understood?

PRINCE. Yes, Mother.

SCENE 2

Enter Awali and Jawali, dancing.

BHAGAVATA. You and I are a great pair of twins,
we two together play and sing,
Awali Jawali, Jawali Awali.
We smile, they all smile; we cry, they all cry.
Those who never laugh will laugh with us,
those who never cry will cry with us,
the laughing pair, the laughing stocks.

AWALI. What sort of a Bhagavata is this? Doesn't he talk to the people who come in?

BHAGAVATA. How should you be addressed?

JAWALI. Hail, brave warrior!

BHAGAVATA. All right, that's what we'll call you. What place are you from?

PRINCE. To whom does Shivapura belong, have you heard?

BHAGAVATA. To the King's mother, Mayavati Devi, so we have heard. Are you she?

JAWALI. No, no! we are . . .

AWALI. Those who make the cosmic egg and all lives that come out of such eggs laugh, or make them cry—the emperors of humour, the laughing stock monarchs, the great twins Awali and Jawali. Do you know who we are?

BHAGAVATA. No notion.

AWALI. That's who we are.

BHAGAVATA. Oh, so you are the twins! Between you two, who is the elder brother and who is the younger one?

JAWALI. I am the elder brother and he is the younger one.

AWALI. No sir, I am the elder brother and he is the younger one.

BHAGAVATA. Is there no agreement between you?

BOTH. I am the elder or the younger brother.

BHAGAVATA. This is like a riddle.

AWALI. Sir, I will ask you a riddle, will you solve it?

BHAGAVATA. What is it?

AWALI. If this is there, that is not there—if that is there, this is not there. What is this, say?

BHAGAVATA. I don't get it.

JAWALI. So you give up?

BHAGAVATA. I give up.

AWALI. When there is a bride, there is no groom, and when there is a groom, there is no bride.

BHAGAVATA. What does that mean?

AWALI. You know the Prince, our friend? There are brides for him, yet if he is asked to marry, he refuses. And when we men want to marry, there are no brides for us.

BHAGAVATA. There is a girl, will you marry her?

BOTH. Oh, yes.

BHAGAVATA. There's only one girl, how can both of you marry her?

AWALI. Oh, you are right. Elder one, Jawali, you get married.

JAWALI. Well, say I got married. Since you resemble me so much, my wife may go to bed with you mistaking you for me. What then? No, no, you marry.

AWALI. What did you say?

JAWALI. The same, as you just said.

AWALI. I said you must marry.

JAWALI. And I said you must.

AWALI (*with anger*). If I had a couple of fangs, I would have sucked your blood. I have spared you because I don't have them.

JAWALI (*with anger*). If I had a couple of horns, I would have run them through your belly. I have spared you because I don't have them.

Meanwhile a woman enters, dancing. Both forget about fighting and stand staring, in a daze.

BHAGAVATA. Who are you lady?

WOMAN. Oh, sir, am I not the one who asked you to look for a bridegroom?

BHAGAVATA. Oh, of course. Now, I remember but I've forgotten your name. What is your name?

WOMAN. Should I say it again? Well listen: Mire is her birthplace. Water is the place of relations. Looking at the man of light, she blooms. Say, what is it?

JAWALI. Shall I say, sir?

BHAGAVATA. Go ahead, my boy.

JAWALI. Mire is your birthplace,
Water of rains, your in-law's place,
Man of light is your lamp.
Blooming one, aren't you?

Your name is Big Frog,
Isn't it? Your name is Big Frog.

All except Jawali laugh.

AWALI. Look, how enthusiastically he exhibits his foolishness. Sorry, sir. Shall I say it?

BHAGAVATA. Yes.

AWALI. She who is born in the mire,
She who floats on water
She who blooms in light
Green Moss, aren't you?
Hey, hey woman! Isn't Green Moss your name?

All except Awali laugh.

BHAGAVATA. Can't you guess this much? Her name is Kamala, the lotus.

AWALI. I knew it sir, but she looks lovely when she laughs, so I said that to make her laugh. (*Kneeling in front of Kamala*) Lady, to this much I swear: I will take the vow of obedient husbandhood forever, and will serve you according to your dictates. This is the aim of my life. Won't you fulfil this wish?

JAWALI. My sacrifice cannot be less than this. Awali, I will sacrifice my very determination for your sake. I will marry her myself, right? Lady, won't you fulfil my wish? (*He too kneels in front of Kamala.*)

AWALI. Why do you repeat all that I say?

JAWALI. That's exactly what I am asking you.

AWALI. You know how angry I am?

JAWALI. How angry?

AWALI. Very, that is, extraordinarily, that is, anger simply boils within me.

JAWALI. Boils? I will boil my grains in it. Please let me.

AWALI. How?

JAWALI. Say what I say. Now let us see. (*Slapping his chest*) Kamala is mine.

AWALI (*slapping his chest*). Kamala is mine.

JAWALI (*pointing Awali's fingers at himself*). Say, she is mine.

AWALI (*pointing Jawali's fingers at himself*). Say, she is mine.

JAWALI. Will you stop this and bark out something else?

AWALI. Will you kindly bark out something else?

JAWALI. I knew sir, that he is neither my elder nor younger brother, that he was a rat or a bandicoot. See how soon he has snapped the cords of brotherhood between the two of us.

AWALI. I knew sir, that he is neither elder brother nor younger, that he is a wolf or a fox. See how he devoured the bond between us. I had decided to see the greatest fraternal disloyalty on earth and then die. I have seen it. I must die now. See you later.

BHAGAVATA. How will you come back to see me after dying?

JAWALI. He will come back somehow to kill me, sir. Hark, if there be any petty deities around, come and save me.

BHAGAVATA. Look, what is this? Do you think Kamala is a lottery? Isn't she the one to decide which of you she wants? Kamala, choose your man.

KAMALA. How is it possible, sir? Both are alike. Let them fight a duel. The winner is my choice, agreed?

AWALI. Agreed. Look, I am ready for the fight. (*To Jawali*) Hey, you huge stray dog, pig . . .

JAWALI. Don't reel out your titles in front of me. Come fight, quick. Now take this. (*Slaps Awali.*)

Awali begins to cry.

AWALI. Ah, ah . . . Oh my family god, save me. If you come here now, grant me this boon, that . . .

JAWALI. Let Kamala be my wife.

KAMALA. Amen. (*She clasps Jawali 's hand.*)

BHAGAVATA. So, it is done. Kamala herself solved the problem. Now, I guess you both can live in peace.

AWALI. How can there be peace now, sir? I will go to the forest, do penance and return a god to bestow the boon of death on both of them. Look, I am going to the forest.

JAWALI. Wait, wait. First see us getting married and only then go, burning with jealousy. Sir Bhagavata, please bless us.

Jawali and Kamala bow to the Bhagavata. He blesses them.

AWALI (*in sorrow*). Hey, sir, one last word.

BHAGAVATA. What is it, son?

AWALI. We have both served the Prince, our friend, till now. Now, I am going to the forest. Ask him if he will carry on the work wholeheartedly. I say all this because when I imagine the Prince without me, helpless and crying out 'Oh friend, Awali' . . . I feel overwhelmed with sorrow.

JAWALI. Tell him, sir, that if he leaves the city immediately, I will serve the Prince with total dedication.

AWALI. It is the Prince's bedtime. Ask him to go and guard the Prince. (*Goes out weeping.*)

JAWALI. Go, elder or younger brother, the river is dry. Fill it up with your tears. Let us see if it will begin to flow.

SCENE 3

Bhagavata and the chorus. The Prince, sleeping, in his room in the Palace.

BHAGAVATA. Thus the Prince in Indranivas Palace
having lain down full of worries
—how can I believe my eyes?—
saw the carved lampstand come to life,
saying 'Beloved', beckoning,
inviting intimacy? Was that the wonder?
From the scabbard came the sword,
that came alive between the thighs.

While the above song is being sung, a statue of a woman bearing a lamp comes to life and starts dancing. The Prince is awakened, and while he attempts to catch the woman, she vanishes, dancing, into him. The Prince is in a state of high rapture.

PRINCE. Oh! What a marvel! Could it be some goddess was under a curse, turned to stone all this time, has now rid herself of the curse and come to life again? Or some nymph who fell in love with me and hid in the stone, waiting for me, has now come out of her stone hiding place and blossomed into life? That creature who kept the burning lamp in her palm and leapt like flashing lightning has dissolved into my body! Is she suggesting that this is how I should get married? Yes, she must be the woman who satisfies all desires, who I have been longing for these many days. If that is so, I have found my bride. Friend, get up! I have found her! (*Stirs Jawali awake.*)

JAWALI (*waking*). You don't even let me sleep, man!

PRINCE. Wake up quickly!

JAWALI. How can I wake up any more than this?

PRINCE. I've found the one.

JAWALI. Who have you found? I'm right here.

PRINCE. Uff! You don't understand me!

JAWALI. Then tell me, man, so I can understand, who is the one you have found? Where is she? Have you hidden her under the bed?

PRINCE. Stop joking. Please listen.

JAWALI. Please speak.

PRINCE. While I was fast asleep, it seemed that the wall of this palace cracked, and someone drew a sword from its scabbard and let my thighs feel its edge. I immediately awoke and sat up, and dreams that were hidden in the corners seemed to spring up before my eyes. Wasn't there a figure of a woman bearing a lamp in that corner? Well, it suddenly filled with life, and its face bloomed with youth, and blossomed with a mysterious smile. While I went on watching it—no, her—she started to dance around me, holding the holy flame in her palm. As she danced, the sight of her flooded my limbs with pleasure and the pleasure became a creeper winding tightly all round my body and blocking my breath, so that I was stumbling, and in this tight embrace she dissolved into me.

JAWALI. It sounds to me from what you say that it must have been the mischief of some female ghost. Dear friend, it would be good for you to keep a metal pot full of water beside your pillow. Do you know what for? So ghosts won't linger near you.

PRINCE. This was no ghost, fellow. How can I tell you? Look, in that corner, there used to be a figure of a maiden with a lamp, do you remember?

JAWALI. Ah! Where has it gone?

PRINCE. Didn't I tell you? It came to life and dissolved into me while dancing. I am still perspiring with wonder. Run straightaway to my mother. Tell her to arrange a meeting of the Elders in the morning.

JAWALI. At least let the morning come, man.

PRINCE. No. Can't you see that it is dawn? Mother is worried. Go immediately, and tell her that the Prince has agreed to marry, with some conditions.

JAWALI. What? You've finally agreed to marry? Who's the beauty?

PRINCE. I'll tell you. First go and tell my mother.

Jawali exits.

SCENE 4

In the Palace: the Queen Mother, the Prince and the Elders.

BHAGAVATA. Elated as she heard the news, the Mother woke, circling, hailed the family god. Soon all were gathered in the court, and the Son arrived like the moon after an eclipse.

QUEEN MOTHER. Body and mind, mangled by horrid dreams, felt all the pleasure of the seven worlds at the news that our son had agreed to marry. On the wave of this pleasure, the Elders of the clan were brought forth to the palace. Thus our royal summons was sent, and none refused to hear it. All have come and are honoured in their respective places. Honoured Elders, our son has agreed to marry. He says he has some conditions. Being a woman, how can we handle this matter? You are equal in our eyes to gods. You, friends, must take care of this matter.

1ST ELDER. We are all happy at this pleasing news, lady. Speak, O Prince, make your desires known to all.

PRINCE. My Elders to me are not distinct from the gods. Your desire is that I should be married, is it not? I agree to do as you desire. For the rest, you should agree to what I desire.

2ND ELDER. We also agree.

PRINCE. It is I who will say which girl is to be my queen.

1ST ELDER. We are agreed.

PRINCE. In whatever form she is, you will get her for me.

2ND ELDER. Wherever the maiden you desire may be, in whatever form she is, it is our responsibility to get her for you.

PRINCE. Do you swear by the family god you will get her?

3RD ELDER. Yes, yes. We swear by the feet of the family god we will get her.

PRINCE. You have sworn. Your words are not different from the prophecies of the gods. Do not ignore my words, thinking me only a boy, but listen carefully.

BHAGAVATA. Split, split my body into equal halves,
chop, chop it into even pieces.
Place at once those pieces in two pots!
Mother, comfort-giving Mother,
after a fortnight with your own eyes—
open, know and all rejoice.

PRINCE. Listen, I'll tell you. With this sword which you see before you, and with the family god as witness, I am to be split into two equal pieces.

QUEEN MOTHER. Shiva, Shiva! Do not utter such inauspicious words, my son!

PRINCE. That is not all. After I have been cut into two, each piece should be stuffed into a pot. Both pots should be buried among flowers. On the next full-moon day, when you open the two pots, you will see come out of one a prince of matchless charm, that is, myself. From the other will come the palace lamp maiden, a woman of statue-like beauty holding a light in her hand. Then you should get the two of us married. If this is agreed, there will be a marriage. If not, no.

2ND ELDER. We have seen many wonders and assimilated them. But of such an unlikely happening we have never heard.

PRINCE. You have sworn before the family god, don't forget.

QUEEN MOTHER. This is madness, my son. Some spirit has entered you to make you act like this.

PRINCE. What entered me was not a spirit, Mother, but a beautiful woman in the form of a lamp bearer. And this is the means by which she who has dissolved into me can be brought out.

QUEEN MOTHER. Can a human being who has been split in half come to life again? Can a woman be brought out of a dead body?

PRINCE. It is possible, Mother. If you have the courage, and if you believe me, I will show you and you will see with your own eyes.

QUEEN MOTHER. Can we play childishly with such things? The Elders of the clan are not common men. Each of them knows a thousand wise sayings. You must act according to their experience.

PRINCE. If the Elders act according to the word they have given, they are the equals of god and the fates. If they do not, they are the equals of human worms. If Mother consents to this, she is the equal of the goddess of creation. If not, she is the equal of the black goddess. If you agree to what I say, there will be a marriage. If not, you will see me leave here as a wandering monk. (*Rushes away*.)

BHAGAVATA. Is the curse coming true, is our family's sin overflowing? Is our acquired merit wasted, has this lineage begun to burn?

QUEEN MOTHER. O Shiva, I never expected that the punishment of fate would so soon leap upon me! Listening to my son's words, my fears were aroused to haunt me. O Elders, you know the history of our lineage from beginning to end. It is your responsibility to protect it.

1ST ELDER. We have heard from legends and histories how one or two kings of this lineage split themselves in two in this way. But now this situation has come about in truth and in our own lifetime! Console yourself, lady! Now you are the one who must take heart and hearten others. We, the Elders, not knowing the mind of the Prince, promised in the presence of god to do as he says. Or perhaps fate itself, unknown to us, made us utter those words. Anyhow, since the Prince has no brother to share his inheritance, there is no fear of his death. Whether your son is to become a monk will be a test of the strength of the family god, will it not, lady?

QUEEN MOTHER. O Elders, I have placed the scion of this family in your hands. Do whatever you will.

SCENE 5

The Queen Mother, Prince and the Elders.

BHAGAVATA. In flowing light, the Elders gathered,
the feet of all the gods were worshipped,
the Prince's body split and buried, then opened.
See, what is this like the sun burning,
a precious gem its hood adorning,
lifting its hood like a big basket as it moves?
Saying 'Careful!' tittering, scattering,
Saying 'Hit it!' 'Kill it!' they attacked it.
Alas! They saw it disappearing into the forest.
Anxiously, the pot remaining
they raised and opened, calling on Shiva.
The smiling Prince, the best of the men, came out.

PRINCE. Where is the lamp maiden?

QUEEN MOTHER. What is this madness, son? Listening to the words of your youthful rashness, we have done many things that we ought not to have done. All this comes from the curse on our lineage. Why else should it happen? By the blessings of the family god, you have come through to a new birth, at least. That is enough.

PRINCE. Why? Did the lamp maiden not come out of the other pot?

1ST ELDER. What came out was a hideous, horrible demon!

2ND ELDER. An evil creature.

1ST ELDER. A ghost.

PRINCE. Cheated!

QUEEN MOTHER. Who is cheated? We are. For having tested thus the family god, we will have to pay a thousand penalties. And now we all must make new marriage arrangements.

SCENE 6

Kamala and Jawali in their house.

KAMALA. Husband, ever since our marriage, you have looked worried. Why?

JAWALI. Marriage? Whose marriage? Mine? The King's? Or Awali's?

KAMALA. Our marriage, that is, yours and mine.

JAWALI. Oh, is that so? My love, last night in my dream, I was comparing you to a bird. But the comparison did not seem right because Awali had, that same night, in his dream, composed a poem in which he compared you to a bird. Please don't think of him too much, because then he appears in your dream.

KAMALA. Husband, about your younger brother . . . why do you . . .

JAWALI. Not younger, elder.

KAMALA. What is Awali to you?

JAWALI. Elder or younger brother.

KAMALA. Well, your elder or younger brother is not here. Why do you hate him so much?

JAWALI. Do I hate him? Impossible! To tell you the truth, you are the apple of one eye and he is of the other. I hold you both equal, you know? Because my elder or younger brother is not beside me, I am so afraid that I don't know what to say.

KAMALA. Look into my eyes. (*He does so.*) Don't you know what to say now?

JAWALI. I do. But today in one of your eyes I see myself and in the other my brother has appeared.

KAMALA (*closing one eye*). Now look, who do you see?

JAWALI. Awali.

KAMALA (*opening the eye she had closed and closing the other*). Now?

JAWALI. Still Awali, even now.

KAMALA. What is he doing?

JAWALI. He is looking at you and sighing.

KAMALA. Awali has become a ghost to worry you.

JAWALI. Not a ghost—a wolf, a hungry wolf.

KAMALA. Then imagine that I am a tiger, and the wolf runs away.

JAWALI. Oh, no, no, you be Kamala. I'm more afraid of the tiger.

KAMALA. You keep talking about Awali, why did you let him go?

JAWALI. I wanted to finish him off. But what to do, the wretch is so much like me, you see, I thought, 'Let me respect myself, at least' and let him go.

KAMALA. O sir, this has gone too far.

BHAGAVATA. What?

KAMALA. You got us married. But instead of making love, all he does is remember his elder or younger brother and pine away for him.

BHAGAVATA. Hey Jawali, I got you married thinking that you were a gentleman. If you go on doing this, I will have to change my opinion of you.

JAWALI. What shall I do, sir? As soon as I look at Kamala with desire, my younger or elder brother appears in both her eyes. If I think of making love with the light off and our eyes closed, I get scared that he, who has hidden in her eyes, may rise up. That is why my eyes sting when I think of love.

BHAGAVATA. But you can't ruin Kamala's life! Today is a Monday. Both of you go and consult your family god.

JAWALI. Not today, the Queen has given me some urgent work to do.

BHAGAVATA. What work?

JAWALI. You must have heard the rumour about how my friend the Prince sneaks out of the palace at odd hours?

BHAGAVATA. We have.

JAWALI. The Queen has asked me to follow the Prince when he sneaks out and find out everything. After I come back, on some other day, we will go and consult the family god. Till then, I pray, keep your good opinion of me.

BHAGAVATA. Well . . .

Jawali and Kamala exit, on opposite sides of the stage.

SCENE 7

The Queen Mother and the Elders in the palace.

BHAGAVATA. Siri Sampige he married
but she could not satisfy him,
everywhere he went searching only for the lamp maiden.
The Prince's ever-growing madness
made his ageing Mother worry,
'What god, what angel can protect our family?
Who'll guard our lineage in the future?
Lovely queen Sampige Devi's
lotus face? How can I bear to look at?'

QUEEN MOTHER. So much we possessed, Elders, and what has become of it? I had hoped to spend the last days of my life gazing on my son as King and head of a family, playing with my grandchildren. How can Shiva punish me so? They say that after marriage a son leaves the mother who bore him and falls under the spell of his bedfellow. No such thing happened here. I have not seen husband and wife laughing together even once. From the first day of their marriage, he would disappear at any time. Come back at any time. He goes off as if searching for something he has lost and returns as if hopeless at not finding what he seeks. He does not talk to anyone. When the family god was consulted, he sobbed and did not open his mouth to say anything. I cannot bear to see the face of my daughter-in-law, who is weeping all the time. My son's face I do not see. Tell me, Elders, what is to be done now?

1ST ELDER. Does the Prince eat from time to time, lady?

QUEEN MOTHER. He eats, he does not eat. When he looks at me, he turns his face away like a guilty person. Is it the family god's anger or the curse or possession by some ghost? I understand nothing.

2ND ELDER. Where does he go, do you know, lady?

QUEEN MOTHER. I don't know, but he returns filthy, as if he has been rolling in mud.

3RD ELDER. Did you consult the astrologers, lady?

QUEEN MOTHER. They say he is haunted by a female spirit. It may be true because, the day before he was split in two, he said that the lamp maiden of Indraniva's Palace had come to life and danced before dissolving into him. What is surprising is that the statue has also vanished since that day.

1ST ELDER. Has the Prince looked at least once at his goddess-like Queen, lady? If he had seen her, this problem would surely not exist.

QUEEN MOTHER. The problem, Elders, is deeper than you realize.

BHAGAVATA. Once, not being able to see the lamp maiden in Siri Sampige's eyes, he said: 'You are not the bride I desire—Go away!'

QUEEN MOTHER. Once, and only once it seems, he started to stare at Siri Sampige's face. When she became shy and covered her face with her hands, apparently, he rushed to her and pulled her hands away and held her face in his palms, fixing his eyes on hers. But at once he said dejectedly, letting go of her face, 'There is no lamp maiden in your eyes, lady', and left her. It is fortunate that the lamp maiden was not to be seen in her eyes. If he had seen her there, he might have plucked the girl's eyes out. Jawali has been sent to follow him in secret, to find out where he goes and what he does. Look, he is coming now.

Jawali enters and falls at the feet of the Queen Mother.

QUEEN MOTHER. Come, son. You must have found out the secret which is still hidden even after many servants have been sent to find it out. Tell me, where is the Prince now? What is he doing? I am eager to hear, in detail. Were you able to follow him to the end?

JAWALI. I was able to follow him, Mother, but what I saw there was terrible.

QUEEN MOTHER. That is what I want to know. Tell me!

BHAGAVATA. Weeping, seeking the lamp maiden,
wandering over hill and mountain
to a pond he came then, thirsty for water.
Oh water, water, say who is she!
Is she not the lamp maiden?
Saying 'I have her', he fell to the tempting reflection.

JAWALI. Last night I followed the Prince, according to your orders. It seemed he was going on a journey without preparations and without saying bidding to anyone. He went in fear, looking behind him, not seeing the way, stumbling, hiding wherever hiding places were to be found. Anyone who had seen him then would have said he was a criminal or convict fleeing, running away. Becoming thirsty, he went to a pond near the forest. The moon was out, and the sky was shining in the pond. Clouds had floated up, and beyond them infinite depths could be seen. He didn't notice that I had stolen up behind him while he looked into the pond. At the touch of his breath, as if angered, the water in the pond trembled and waves rose and broke up the reflected clouds and the deep-blue sky seemed to be sliced by cruel knives. But my friend and the Prince did not draw back. Until the play of the water was finished, he remained still, and then again he looked at himself in the water. His reflection came up there like a floating corpse. The moment he saw it, his face shone. Tears of happiness came to his eyes. In his ecstasy no word came from his mouth. As if silently talking with that corpse, he sat there, still.

QUEEN MOTHER. Strange! And then?

JAWALI. He caught the reflection in his cupped hands and looked at it. The water spilled out between his fingers. Again he caught it and again it spilled. Then, as if the whole forest were crying, he raised his voice saying 'Maiden, Maiden!' and wept.

QUEEN MOTHER. Did he say 'Maiden'?

JAWALI. Yes.

QUEEN MOTHER. Did he weep?

JAWALI. Yes, Mother.

QUEEN MOTHER. Listening to your tale has made me afraid, son. What should not have happened, what I was guarding against for sixteen years, has happened now, out of my sight. The only difference is that he, who should have become a monk on seeing his reflection, is now thinking of the lamp maiden.

1ST ELDER. This is a strange madness, one never seen or heard or before. There is no doubt about it.

2ND ELDER. Have people lived who have loved their reflection in the water like this?

QUEEN MOTHER. My daughter-in-law is a thousand times prettier than that reflection, is she not?

3RD ELDER. Reason cannot give an answer to madness, lady. The Prince, in the bloom of youth, succumbed rapidly to the fascination of that woman. The right thing to do will be to wait and see, lady. The Prince is coming, madam.

QUEEN MOTHER. Let him come. Jawali, you two are boyhood friends. You can open your minds to each other. Try to find out the reason for his madness.

JAWALI. Very well, Mother.

All exit except Jawali. The Prince enters. On seeing Jawali, he is disturbed.

PRINCE. What is it? Why are you looking at me like that?

JAWALI. It's nothing.

PRINCE. I've gone mad—that's what you think, isn't it? But I can tell you that this is definitely not madness. My difficulty is that I cannot prove that all of you are cheats.

JAWALI. Cheats? How have we cheated you?

PRINCE. You said there was no lamp maiden anywhere.

JAWALI. Yes. She wasn't found.

PRINCE. So you say I was lying.

JAWALI. Not lying . . . but she's nowhere to be seen.

PRINCE. Yet she exists. Do you know I go out every day and see her?

JAWALI. Do you really? Tell me all about it.

PRINCE. You won't tease me?

JAWALI. Do you doubt even your friend?

BHAGAVATA. She came floating on the water,
beauty in the waves swimming—
could I cast a fishing line and pull her in?
Slowly, slowly, in the play of
ripples I saw the goal I was seeking.

PRINCE. In that case, listen. Today I was beside a pond. She was inside it. She was swimming in the waves and ripples, glittering like a fish, moving her tiny arms. 'I must cast a line to catch her,' I thought. 'No,' I thought, 'I can catch her in my hand,' and I stretched out my cupped hands. When my breath touched the water in my hands—do you know—she trembled for love? Slowly she dripped down again between my fingers. Saying 'Silly girl!' I pinched her cheek. She laughed—do you know—like lines running in the waves. Seeing her I laughed too, and I spoke. She spoke also. Everything I did she did too, or everything she did I did too, there was so much harmony between the two of us that, like two halves coming together, we had become one. Gradually we became, both together, an indivisible zero, transcending form, becoming the Shivalinga, becoming god. Nor did the shadow of imperfect sorrow linger around this new god. Both of us together became this new god—ah!—it was like air, it was like light, it was like the blue of the sky, it was like empty space—it seemed it was impossible for anything physical to touch him. After seeing that god, I realized what beauty is and what ugliness is. Suddenly I felt that there is something lacking in this world we live in. Ah, god! It is a puzzle how we go on living with so much lack.

JAWALI. Friend, is that god just sprouting a moustache?

PRINCE. Yes.

JAWALI. And is there a dark mole on his right cheek?

PRINCE. Yes. How did you know?

JAWALI. How could I not know? What you saw was your own reflection.

PRINCE. Ay! Blast my foolishness in arguing with an ignorant person like you. Seeing one's reflection and becoming one with it means seeing the shape of the soul. But you can't understand all this. You are stuck to the body. People who refuse to see any further than the body cannot understand such things.

JAWALI. To me 'body' means an empty stomach, and 'soul' means a full stomach. What do you say?

PRINCE. What? Are you teasing me?

The Prince looks for some time at Jawali, annoyed at his apparent teasing, then goes off dejectedly. Jawali follows him.

SCENE 8

Enter Kalinga.

BHAGAVATA. Ask not where he went—the Serpent
has made its dwelling deep inside you,
go not searching for your lost one
living deep inside the anthill of the mind (*To Kalinga*)
Bravo, sustainer of the serpent lineage!

KALINGA. Who does the nether world belong to, do you know?

BHAGAVATA. We have heard it is Lord Kalinga.

KALINGA. We are that lord.

BHAGAVATA. For what reason do we suddenly see you here?

KALINGA. Aahaaah! We the traveller and acclaimed great hero of the eight directions and the fourteen worlds were resting after our daily duties in our palace in the nether world, when a girl's voice appeared to be calling us. While we were wondering how a woman's voice could be making itself heard in a bachelor's palace, as if descending to plunder our world she appeared before us. Losing all sense of ourselves, we knelt before her. Was it a dream or was it real? Such a thing might perhaps occur once in a while, but that was not the case here—every day we saw the same vision. Why should we be thinking about a woman who belongs to someone else? But that also did not seem to be the case. She seemed to be our rightful wife, known to us for a long time. From the day we saw her, the desire to possess her stirred in us. Very well. We decided to go in search of her.

Sampige appears.

BHAGAVATA. Oho! Is this the lovely beauty,
she who appeared to us in visions?
If she won't be mine, my life is wasted—
till my dying breath I cannot give her up.

KALINGA. Aahaah! So where was she, the girl who seduced my mind? I went about searching every region of the earth, but she is finally found here in the backyard of Indranivas Palace in Shivapura. There she is, the girl over there. She's the one who stole my mind away! Even at this distance, the smell of ploughed earth that her body exhales makes me tingle. Aha! She is not an easy woman. She must be the prettiest in the province! All right. I will go up to her and make myself visible.

BHAGAVATA. Who is this, that comes riding up
my body, who is he that I
don't know, yet upon my mind
is printed?
Wherever I go, I see arise
and stand by me, his handsome shape,
and longings of desire are born
to trouble me.

SAMPIGE. Who is he? As if the five elements came together and took shape, he came walking from the direction of the anthill. For quite some time, he has been chasing me. Wherever I go, he is looking at me with hungry eyes. Wherever he steps, sparks seem to fly. I do not know him, but he appears to be etched on mind, and as I see his handsome form, my desire rises. Longings I had not known before are now standing with their mouths open. Who is he?

BHAGAVATA. Pleased as if he's found a treasure
Kalinga, swollen proud and vain,
says: Whether she is maid or wife,
she must be mine, I'll plunder all
her joys.

KALINGA. Aha! Her body is like a festival for my aroused senses. It seems to be beckoning. Big buttocks, big big breasts! Small waist, pool of pleasure! Eyes trained in hunting. Whether she's maid or wife, even if my life is lost in the attempt, it doesn't matter. Unless I bed her, my life has been wasted.

BHAGAVATA. One must not yield to base desires—
it's fitting to advise him so.
He ran up, she stopped him, but she looked,
and fell under the wizard's spell.

SAMPIGE. I have become like a boat caught in a storm and overturned. Someone is opening the doors of my youthful breast, and shaking all my desires to awaken them. No, I must not sacrifice my judgement to such base desires. I will talk with that man who is coming to seduce a woman belonging to another, scold him and send him away.

(*She goes a little further forward and hides. Kalinga goes running towards her. Sampige closes the door and stands at the door.*)

Who are you that chooses a time when no one is near and comes to chase me wherever I go? It is the Queen of this country herself who you are provoking! You must be a shameless rogue to dare as much!

KALINGA. Aha, your voice is like honey, my lovely. Your angry words sound sweet. You make me want to catch and kiss the words as they are born from your mouth.

SAMPIGE. Answer the question I asked you. If you try any mischief, I'll tell the King, and he'll have you chained and dragged through the streets.

KALINGA. You have already bound up my heart and mind with your long hair, girl. The only thing left is for you to put chains on my body with your smooth arms. And I am prepared for that.

SAMPIGE. The intoxication of youth has gone to your head. It seems you don't understand civilized words. Wait. (*She shouts*) Mother!

KALINGA. You are a good actress. When I came, you shut the door, and now you are pretending to call someone to protect you. Your kind of woman finds force very attractive, I know. So here you are!

QUEEN MOTHER (*from outside*). Siri Sampige!

SAMPIGE. The Queen Mother has come. If you want to live, hide!

KALINGA. Don't talk so proudly. I can protect myself. If you have any courage, open the door!

SAMPIGE. My virtue is in my own hands. Who should I fear? Look, I am opening the door. Guard yourself.

Sampige opens the door. The Queen Mother enters. Kalinga immediately changes shape, becomes the King.

QUEEN MOTHER. What a surprise. Husband and wife together and happy! Day and night I do penance to bring that about! Son, on my eyes dried up from joylessness, you have showered the rain of a new joy. Wait, wait! I will straightaway make a sacrifice of an eight-legged animal to the family god. Son, Siri Sampige is very delicate. Do not make her shout again with your roughness, do you hear?

KALINGA (*resting his arm on Sampige's shoulders; she moves away*). We'll tame her. Don't worry, Mother. Sampige only called you for fun, didn't you, my goddess?

SAMPIGE. Yes. No, no, I really called. (*Aside*) So much joy wells up in me at his touch. Who is this wizard who has come to plunder me?

QUEEN MOTHER. Son, stop your roughness. Siri Sampige is already trembling like a flowering creeper.

KALINGA. What is an eight-legged animal, Mother?

QUEEN MOTHER. It means a pregnant animal. I will sacrifice one so that our Siri Sampige will quickly give me a grandson. In the pools of her eyes I can already see suffused and shining the golden colour of tomorrow's dream. If you stand here like this, my evil eye may fall on my dear daughter-in-law. Close the door. (*Exits.*)

SAMPIGE. Before madness overcomes me, please tell me who you are. You were like a hissing snake, and now you are like the Prince. How many existences do you have?

KALINGA. As many as you want. Look into my eyes, girl. Am I like your Prince?

SAMPIGE. True. The Prince is a little effeminate to look at.

KALINGA. A little! Quite a lot.

SAMPIGE. It was to search for the woman inside him that he split himself, wasn't it?

KALINGA. In that case, now tell me—am I a stranger? While you were in bed with your husband who was lying there like a piece of wood, was there not in the nether regions of your mind a king kneeling before you, begging for your love?

SAMPIGE. Yes.

KALINGA. That was me. Did you recognize me as King Kalinga, ruler of the nether world in the depths of the Prince's palace?

SAMPIGE. Yes. No, no. I don't know who you are.

KALINGA. But I know you. I can even tell you what dreams you dream. And I will teach you the dreams that you shall have from today on. Come on now, dreams, let us see. There is a forest, and in the forest there are flowers, tender leaves, trees full of fruit . . .

SAMPIGE. Yes, there is a forest, there are fruit trees . . .

KALINGA. In fresh sunlight, a golden river is flowing.

SAMPIGE. A river is flowing. You have come to fetch water.

SAMPIGE. Yes, I have come to fetch water. Here in the ground there is an entrance like a burrow.

KALINGA. Descend.

SAMPIGE. Aah! How fine this world is. How many coffers of gold there are in the nether regions. In every corner, so many nameless joys are sleeping freely. Ay! a seven-hooded snake is standing like a lampstand, aiming its raised hoods at me. What can I do?

KALINGA (*taking his true form*). Don't be afraid, girl. I am yours.

SCENE 9

Jawali and Bhagavata.

JAWALI. Hey, Bhagavata!

BHAGAVATA. What?

JAWALI. Shut one eye and look at me.

BHAGAVATA. I looked.

JAWALI. How many people am I?

BHAGAVATA. Only one.

JAWALI. All right, now open both eyes and look at me. How many people am I, tell me.

BHAGAVATA. Only one.

JAWALI. What, Bhagavata, sir! You are making fun of me. If with one eye we see one man, with both eyes we should see two men.

BHAGAVATA. Is that so? In that case, how many people do I look like to your eyes?

JAWALI. Two.

BHAGAVATA. How?

JAWALI. You and I. You and your shadow. Awali and I. That's why I sometimes feel as if I had four legs. Don't you, Bhagavata?

BHAGAVATA. You are lucky and I am unlucky. I have only two legs.

JAWALI. You are also lucky, Bhagavata, sir. Do you want to know why? In front of you, let us assume that there are two paths. By keeping one leg on each, you can walk down both paths.

BHAGAVATA. Bravo, bravo! We did not know that at all. So you walk down four paths at the same time, do you?

JAWALI. I? No, Bhagavata, sir, but I have seen with my own eyes, Bhagavata, one man walking at the same time down two paths.

BHAGAVATA. Is that so? Who is that fortunate person?

JAWALI. Our Prince. He is to be found with the Queen in the women's apartments. At the same time he is to be found near the pond as before, looking at the god reflected in the water.

BHAGAVATA. How can that be?

JAWALI. Think of my position! At times he recognizes me, at other times he turns his face away like a stranger. If I see him in the women's apartments, he becomes confused and asks me 'Who are you?' If I go to the pond, he calls me 'friend' and embraces me. If I tell him, 'You didn't recognize me in the palace, friend,' he says 'I didn't go to the palace at all!' Let's say that one hand may not know what the other hand is doing, but isn't it strange that one leg doesn't know the path that the other is walking?

BHAGAVATA. It is strange.

JAWALI. When I told him, 'The Queen is going to have a child, you will soon be the father of a prince, you should give your poor friend a tasty dinner of game,' his eyes widened and he looked at me as if he would tear me apart and devour me!

BHAGAVATA. What joyful news you bring! The Queen has become pregnant! Couldn't he at least have handed out sweets to me, the Bhagavata?

JAWALI. Of course, I have brought them, sir, take this. Keep distributing them to all who pass by. I will go and get the things for worship.

BHAGAVATI. Why things for worship?

JAWALI. Look, the very lotus of my heart has bloomed and is approaching us. Ask her.

Jawali goes out, Kamala comes in. Awali who has entered from the back stands unseen.

BHAGAVATA. What is this, Kamala? Are you on your way to offer worship? What is the matter?

KAMALA. Sir Bhagavata, though it is years since we married, my lord, my husband does not love me. Without love, how can there be its fruit, a son, the boon of progeny? I leaned on the pillars of my house, a month on each, sighing and crying out to god. Just the day before yesterday, we were blessed with the grace of the family god. He appeared in my dream and instructed me in this manner:'My daughter, on the anthill, under the banyan tree, outside the city, there is a creeper of blooming jasmines. If you first worship, then pluck the flowers, make a garland out of them and put it round your husband's neck, he will transform himself into a serpent and unite with you. If you unite in this manner, you shall have children, not otherwise.' So we are going there now.

BHAGAVATA. Well, may your wish be fulfilled.

As she leaves, Awali steps in front of her.

AWALI. Lady, I have a request.

KAMALA. What, you are still standing here! Did you get the bael leaf?

AWALI. But you never asked me to.

KAMALA. Look, the old madness again. Now, will you get the leaf or not?

AWALI. But there is no bael tree nearby.

KAMALA. Husband, isn't there a bael tree near the east-side window of our house?

AWALI. Which is the east window of our house?

He goes off, searching. Jawali enters from the other side with the leaf in his hand.

KAMALA. Now, where did it come from? Well, well, no need to explain, get the fruits and flowers.

JAWALI. Oh, sure.

He goes out, Awali enters.

AWALI. Look, the bael leaf.

KAMALA. But you've brought that already, what I asked for were fruits and flowers.

AWALI. OK, I'll get them.

As he leaves, Jawali enters from the opposite side. Seeing both of them standing face to face, Kamala becomes alarmed.

BOTH. Hey, there is a mirror in front of me.

Both act as the object and the image.

AWALI. Mirror, mirror, have you an eye, too?
Or, has my eye become a mirror now?

JAWALI. Is that you seeing me?
Or, is this I seeing you?

AWALI. Am I your image? A shade?
Or are you my image? A shade?

JAWALI. Without me you are not there, is this true?
Or, without you I am not there, is this true?

AWALI. Apart we two may be,
Yet, down below the tree's root is one.

JAWALI. Between us is glass.
When broken, the two ends and we are one.

AWALI. If two ends, do you get one?
Or, is it lonely we get?

JAWALI. Melting, in each other,
Can we live, in the mind doesn't the glass remain?

AWALI. The words we have heard till now . . .

JAWALI. You tell me! A dialogue or a soliloquy?

BOTH (*recognizing each other*). Aren't you my elder or younger brother?

AWALI. How are you, my elder younger brother?

JAWALI. Kamala, go in immediately. I will speak to him and come in.

BHAGAVATA. Oh, isn't one of you two Awali? Are you here too, Awali? What were you doing all these days?

JAWALI. He has done the worst possible things. (*To Awali*) Will you go away now or shall I have a go at all that fat in you?

AWALI. I have as much of a right as you have to both this house and Kamala.

JAWALI (*to Bhagavata*). Tell him Bhagavata Sir, that he is like a bear rushing into the shrine when worship in going on.

AWATI (*to Bhagavata*). Tell him Bhagavata Sir, that he is the zenith of stupidity.

BHAGAVATA. But look, I am confused myself. I don't know, which of you two is Awali and which Jawali. To whom shall I say anything? Lady Kamala, you tell me, which is your husband?

KAMALA. I am confused too. Suggest a means to find this out.

BHAGAVATA. Well then, do this. Our elders used to say that the hearts of those in love beat faster. Hold your ear near both their hearts. The one whose heart beats faster is your husband.

Kamala does so.

KAMALA. Both their hearts are beating like your drums, sir.

JAWALI. All right, let another duel decide this. You, you fox, who come slinking in to chew up the sugarcane in my garden, I am ready to hunt you. Take this, face it.

AWALI (*stepping back in fear*). Why should a duel always decide?

JAWALI (*triumphant*). My love, do you know how replete with virtues of valour and fearlessness I am? Or should I give you a taste of it, too?

KAMALA. I know now, my lord.

JAWALI. Then come now for worship, towards the anthill.

Kamala and Jawali go out.

BHAGAVATA. You went to perform penance, didn't you?

AWALI. I went. I performed the penance, too. After seeing god, I came back.

BHAGAVATA. Really? How is god? Doing well?

AWALI. God means a huge, big firepit of arrogance. He is arrogant because the atoms of dust and blades of grass, even the sun and moon are under his control. Devotees keep pouring the ghee of devotion and the pit keeps glittering with fire. You know, sometimes there are contests between the emperors and god. I thought this very petty and came back here.

BHAGAVATA. Lucky man. You had a great enlightenment.

AWALI. Sir, I want a buffalo. Is there one in your chorus?

BHAGAVATA. There are many in the city. Why do you want a buffalo?

AWALI. I need a pot of milk.

BHAGAVATA. Why milk?

AWALI. To give my brother food, make him eat a gummy plum and drink up that milk. (*Exits.*)

SCENE 10

BHAGAVATA. The god who showed smiling
in the water dripping from cupped hands
has gone back to the depths.
The Prince is stunned.
When he came with empty hands,
the body that was revealed he did not recognize,
and asked 'Who are you, rogue?'

Prince enters, desperate.

PRINCE. Whatever I touch becomes foolishness, whatever I look at becomes deception. It has reached the point where even the clown is laughing at me.

Siri Sampige enters.

SAMPIGE. You look grief stricken, my lord.

PRINCE. Yes. Believing I was certain to see the god, I went out with a light burning in my eyes, but I have returned in darkness. I thought that god may give us pain enough to make us cry, but now all forces have joined in the mischief of darkness so as not to allow any light to come near me.

SAMPIGE. You may have refused my love, but look, my arms are still wide open to receive you, leaving the past behind.

PRINCE. How innocent your face is, my lady. It is, a freshly blossoming lotus without a speck of mire on it, your face. But look at my face. As I pictured the god in the water, the mire below was thrown up at it. The body is pure, my lady, but the soul is dirty. Sins are visible to the soul.

SAMPIGE. You need rest, my lord. If you sleep a little while, and have beautiful dreams . . .

PRINCE. So I should still close my eyes, is that what you suggest! Well, you have dreams, you are fortunate. In reality you are a Queen, and in dreams you are a lover. You can handle the selves of two worlds. But I—the day I was deceived by the god, I lost my dreams too, lady.

SAMPIGE. What does that mean, my lord?

PRINCE. Rejecting my body, leaving it with you, I went to the pond to see the god. What came floating in the water was neither the lamp maiden nor a god. It was not even my reflection, my lady, it was my corpse. And that was what I held daily on my lap and ate of. The more I ate, the hungrier I felt. I ate more and more of it, and by the time I realized it was a corpse, it was too late. When I repented and came back, my body itself had vanished. In the meantime, someone had entered it and gone off with it. Now I am almost air, lady, I cannot even make your skin feel my touch. I don't exist except as air that speaks. I need a body to show myself in. My hunger for life is growing. Lady, I need a body. Please help me.

SAMPIGE. I am a slave at your feet, my lord.

PRINCE. I don't want that. If you help me sincerely, that is enough. Can't you cooperate with me?

SAMPIGE. Of course I will, my lord.

PRINCE. You must not break your word.

SAMPIGE. No, my lord.

PRINCE. Are you sure?

SAMPIGE. Yes.

PRINCE. Will you swear on my life?

SAMPIGE. I swear on your life.

PRINCE. Then look! (*Shouting*) Hey! Who is there?

SAMPIGE. All are sleeping, my lord, who will come?

PRINCE. It is the King of this country himself calling.

SAMPIGE. It is midnight, my lord.

PRINCE. But a great truth has been revealed to the King of the country at this moment. Who is there?

SAMPIGE. If anyone hears, what will they say? Stop it, my lord.

PRINCE. You are a partner in this truth. Be quiet. Who is there?

The Queen Mother and a servant enter.

SERVANT. What are your orders, Your Majesty?

PRINCE. Come, Mother. Servant, go now without delay and beat the drums. I know it is midnight, but do not argue with me. Go and proclaim that tomorrow morning all the citizens and heads must assemble in the Nagalinga temple. Queen Sampige Devi will undergo a trial.

Exit servant.

SAMPIGE. Trial? Why?

PRINCE. To reveal the truth of your illicit pregnancy.

QUEEN MOTHER. Prince, you are not in possession of your senses. Before whom are you speaking thus?

PRINCE. Before my mother, who believes the Queen's lies, and before Queen Sampige Devi herself.

QUEEN MOTHER. Siri Sampige has told no lies.

PRINCE. Please forgive my irreverence, Mother. That foetus in her womb is not mine. To whom does that poison belong? That is the truth that must come out.

QUEEN MOTHER. I say that it is yours.

PRINCE. That is not true, Mother. It's deception.

QUEEN MOTHER. How sure can I be of the truth? If it is true that you are my son, then it is equally true that the child in that womb is yours.

PRINCE. How many truths are you handling, Mother? I cannot manage even one. Since that foetus bears my name, I have the last word, Mother.

QUEEN MOTHER. You are half-mad. You are not fit to bear witness.

PRINCE. That is why I said it should be decided in public.

QUEEN MOTHER. Your madness is spreading beyond all limits. Now you are making a private affair into a public issue.

PRINCE. Before the law all are equal, Mother.

QUEEN MOTHER. This is the height of insanity. (*Painfully*) My eyelids are heavy with the weight of life. Son, I can bear no more.

PRINCE. I too have grown old, Mother. It seems I was always two, and the one that I have lost somewhere must be my elder brother or my enemy. You have kept hidden from me the secret of his existence, like this one, keeping her secret in her womb and wrapping her sari round it. Perhaps you did the same.

QUEEN MOTHER. Prince, no such great catastrophe has happened. Do not lose your judgement in unnecessary hatred.

PRINCE. Even my hatred is split in two, Mother. I cannot wholly hate the Queen. And he who in my absence illicitly was joined with her, who brought a treasure without anyone knowing and hid it in her womb—I have no wholehearted hatred for him either, Mother. Admiration, and jealousy, yes, but I need him. That is why tomorrow morning the Queen's deception must be exposed. As King I have announced it. Tomorrow morning you too must graciously attend. (*Rushes off.*)

SCENE 11

In the temple of Nagalinga: Bhagavata, the Queen Mother, Sampige, the Prince and the Elders.

BHAGAVATA. Honouring the great men who attended
the King bowed and said thus:
'Breaking palace laws Sampige's womb
has quickened. Say, is it right?'

PRINCE. To you, the great of the earth, my devout salutations and thanks for your attendance!

1ST ELDER. We are flattered by your modesty, lord!

PRINCE. In my inexperience, I am facing a dilemma regarding social duty. So I was obliged to call on you, the equals of gods, to guide me.

2ND ELDER. Even the family god will be touched by the decisions that the King takes in the presence of the Elders. We will conscientiously say what is true and right. Please speak, lord.

PRINCE. What should be the punishment for a woman who has abandoned her husband, has illicitly joined with another and become pregnant by him? Let the final word be said.

1ST ELDER. First of all it must be proved that the pregnancy is illicit, lord.

PRINCE. And what is the evidence to prove this?

2ND ELDER. The inmost conscience of husband and wife is the evidence.

PRINCE. And if there are people who can deceive even this inmost conscience?

1ST ELDER. Then the final proof is a trial by ordeal, the form of which is to be decided before all.

PRINCE. In that case, decide. The woman who has committed a crime here, and is illicitly pregnant, is the Queen of the country, and the one who is asking for justice is the King.

All are shocked.

1ST ELDER. O Prince, we have heard you are not in good health. If that is so, it is natural for your mind also to be disturbed. A problem of family prestige such as this can be solved before the Queen Mother, who is like the family god to us all. This is not a public problem. This is our feeling.

PRINCE. When citizens require justice, the King provides justice. When justice for the King is needed, the Elders should provide justice. That is social duty.

2ND ELDER. The King rules over two realms. One is the earth, the other is his wife. So the final authority with regard to justice or injustice in both is his.

PRINCE. Since in the eyes of justice all are equal, and the King himself is in need of justice, I am requesting you to decide. If you still hesitate, it is against your Elder status.

2ND ELDER. You should not force the disturbance of your body and mind upon the Elders, lord. There is still time. You can consult with the Queen Mother and thus take a proper decision. This we humbly pray you to do.

PRINCE. What is the proof that my body and mind are disturbed?

QUEEN MOTHER. The unspeakable words you are saying is that not enough? The soot you are throwing on the history of our family—is that not enough? You are the owner of the body and the mind of the Queen. Not being able to answer for both—is that not enough?

PRINCE. My words are the words of sorrow of one who has suffered an injustice. Don't you understand?

1ST ELDER. Your intervention with your advice, lady, is what will serve best here. Once, some time ago, becoming witnesses to the splitting of the Prince, we allowed our eyes and minds to be wounded. We are not prepared now, in witnessing this madness, to be wounded in our souls. Look, we depart.

PRINCE. You are forbidden in the name of the family god to take one step forward.

2ND ELDER. For the misfortune of being Elders, must we also become partners in all your sins?

QUEEN MOTHER. Keeping in mind the truth of the gods, I pray before all the clan for fortune to favour us. Great efforts must be made to protect the truth, Elders. If we neglect it even for one moment, the truth will fly out of our hands, and this thousand-year-old lineage will collapse. To the man who gives up his judgement for his pride—forgetting his proper destiny and his duty—to this kind of man it is difficult to discern a woman's truth. If everybody's truth was to be at the level of their own noses, what would happen? Fortunately it is not so. Elders like you are here to give a discerning judgement. That is our good fortune. Knowing that this is an insult to a woman, still I insist. The blessings of the family god will prove my daughter-in-law's truthfullness. Please see the trial and give your judgement. Afterwards perhaps my son's madness will be cured.

1ST ELDER. We have no doubts in accepting the Queen Mother's judgement. Let the Prince accept also that there is to be no second opinion about our judgement.

PRINCE. I agree.

2ND ELDER. In that case, listen. Our words are the words of gods. Let the Queen herself decide what the form of the trial should be. We have faith in the Queen's wisdom.

BHAGAVATA. The king cobra writhing in play
on the linga I will take on my body.
If I am pure, it will go away,
otherwise it will sting me.
Do you agree?

SAMPIGE. Look, that snake which is crawling there on the Nagalinga—I will let it climb on my body. If I am a pure and virtuous wife, it will move over my body without stinging me and go away. Otherwise it will use its poison. By this trial, the truth can be tested and punishment be given at the same time. Is it acceptable?

ELDERS. We accept.

QUEEN MOTHER. Come, daughter.

BHAGAVATA. With hands joined above her head
she came before the snake linga
bowed and trod devoutly round the idol.
Abandoning fear, she stretched out her arms;
saying 'Snake, protect the truth,
come to me,' she took the snake upon her body.
Were they friends, she and the snake?
Did the dumb creature know the truth?
Showering the Queen with kisses, charming,
opening its hood it played on her,
the light in its hood-jewels gleaming,
happily twined with her plait, her womb caressing

turned its hood-light to the front
slipped down the slope of her thighs
and seeking its linga master moved away.
All the people stood like painted beings.
'A strange thing we saw,' they said,
'Truth depicted by the Queen's grace for us all.
Hail, oh hail, to our godlike Queen!
Hail to a mother's faithful womb!
Hail to the lineage!'
All bowed to Sampige.

The Prince rushes up to the Nagalinga, but the snake is no longer there. He searches for it, then stands amazed.

QUEEN MOTHER. By showing us this miracle, Siri Sampige has become an angel.

3RD ELDER. What you have done, my lady, has spread the glory of earth up to the Heavens. Our country is blessed.

1ST ELDER. A hundred salutations to the Queen. A thousand victories to the Queen's truth. Wherever the Queen's feet step, may towns and temples rise.

All join their hands in a salute and go up to the Mother, bowing. With the Mother, they go to salute Sampige. Then all exit. Only the Prince remains behind.

PRINCE. This is cheating, cheating!

SCENE 12

Bhagavata, Awali and the Prince.

BHAGAVATA. Without the elder, the younger brother died.

> 'Life has no meaning any more;
> from now on I cannot live,' Awali said and wept.

AWALI (*crying*). Alas! My younger or elder brother is dead! Now I am a-alo-o-one. I no longer have any near or dear ones. Oh god!

PRINCE. Who is that weeping so terribly?

AWALI. I, Awali.

PRINCE. Why are you weeping all alone?

AWALI. Because I am alone, that's why.

PRINCE. Where did Jawali go?

AWALI. He went and died on me.

PRINCE. He died? When? What happened?

AWALI. You know that anthill under the banyan tree outside the city? Well, he had gone there with Kamala to worship.

BHAGAVATA. Inspired by greed, this man too went there with a pot of milk and lay in wait.

AWALI. Not that, I went to bathe the Shivalinga with milk.

PRINCE. And then?

AWALI. After worship, Kamala took the jasmine garland on the linga and put it round Jawali's neck. As soon as she garlanded him, Jawali turned into a serpent.

PRINCE. Don't lie.

AWALI. I'm not lying. Ask this Bhagavata if you want.

BHAGAVATA. It is true that Jawali turned into a serpent. The family god had instructed thus.

AWALI. As soon as he became a serpent, he began the love play with Kamala. Later, he even proceeded to do things, which, out of shame, I can't mention. Gradually, with accelerated pleasure, they both began to pant like flood water rushing down into a valley. To cater to the fatigued and hungry ones, I made a small fire and put the milk on to boil. The milk got heated and started to boil. The boiled milk began to overflow. The smell of the overflowing milk reached the serpent inside Kamala. The serpent came out. Since he was hungry, he spread his hood and dipped his mouth right into the pot. His mouth was burnt and he died, writhing.

BHAGAVATA. Sheer lies, my lord. He killed Jawali.

AWALI. Maybe. But I did so because I felt that he would kill Kamala, lying speechless there.

BHAGAVATA. A lie again. Blinded by jealousy and anger, seizing the opportunity, you chopped the writhing snake whose mouth was burnt with an axe.

AWALI (*weeping*). Alas, I killed my elder or younger brother with my own hands.

PRINCE. Don't cry. Tell me what happened after that. What did Sampige do?

AWALI. Not Sampige, Kamala. Through the horrors she lay still, her eyes closed in intoxicated pleasure. I filled the pots with the serpent bits and threw it out. I cleaned up the blood, woke up Kamala and told her sweetly, 'Come, let us go home.' She thought I was Jawali and began to walk with me. Slowly, she walked a few steps and then sat down saying she was tired. After a while she got up to walk. Gosh, what do I see! She had laid an egg where she had sat down. Angry, because it was the serpent progeny, I crushed it between my hands.

BHAGAVATA. You did that out of your jealousy for Jawali. The one who has seen it seems to know better than the one who has done it. Well, you describe everything, then.

PRINCE. Tell, sir.

BHAGAVATA. He crushed the second egg too in the same manner. But when he crushed even the third, Kamala came to know. As soon as she knew, the contentment and pleasure in her eyes disappeared and she began to tremble with anger enough to fill the seven worlds. The pearl ornament on her nose split into bits. Milk streamed down from her breasts like tears and her blouse became wet. Screaming in a terrible voice and shouting, 'Wretch, you have destroyed my progeny,' she tore her loosened hair, threw it at him and disappeared into the forest. Even the sun set.

AWALI (*weeping*). Oh, alas, I have become lonely now . . .

PRINCE. Don't cry. You also wanted him to be killed, didn't you?

AWALI. Yes.

PRINCE. He's dead and gone. Isn't it better for you?

AWALI. As long as he was here, I wanted to kill him. He was always here or there, behind or in front of me, near or far from me. But now without him I have become half myself. That's why I feel I too should die. I am alone.

PRINCE. Hey, Prince!

AWALI. Prince?

PRINCE. Don't get frightened. I thought you were I. You a fortunate, at least you are alone. Look at me. Even when I am sitting alone, I feel there is someone like me sitting next to me, wandering around in my body, talking in my voice, stealing me. I thought it was not a man but a mirror, but he is not a mirror, because a mirror cannot talk, and he talks. A mirror will not move by itself, but he wanders all through the palace, not caring about me. I will tell you a secret, don't tell anybody. He has stolen my wife also, and slipped into her bed. Wait! Did you hear? His voice from the women's apartments of the palace?

AWALI. Yes, I hear the voice of some man in the women's apartments.

PRINCE. Don't make any noise. The Queen is bathing his face with the light of her eyes, washing away the stains of his sin, thinking that their last moments together should be pure. But I suffer day and night remembering their sins, and roam longing and thirsting for his blood.

AWALI. Shall I bring servants to catch the enemy?

PRINCE. Go! But bring them without making a sound.

SCENE 13

The palace: Sampige nursing the child. Kalinga watching.

BHAGAVATA. Siri Sampige's child I'll go and see,
talk to it and return, said the Snake King.
He crossed the fence and was there.

KALINGA. Won't you speak, Sampige?

SAMPIGE. Why have you come? The Prince suspects me. He doesn't go to the pond any more but guards me like a servant. Don't you understand?

KALINGA. I had to speak to you.

SAMPIGE. Well, you've spoken to me.

KALINGA. I wanted to see the child's face.

SAMPIGE. Look at the child's face. Now you can go.

KALINGA. Just one moment. Give me a chance to talk to you once more, Sampige. Look what has happened to me. My eyes have had no sleep. I do not know where the boundaries of my kingdom are. I just sit around, forgetfully wondering 'Will she look at me once at least?' The walls of the fortress you have built to keep me out are growing taller.

SAMPIGE. I also have my responsibilities and my honour, Kalinga. Please go away.

KALINGA. Remember, my goddess. Remember the dark boy who played with your hair. Sometimes you would say, 'Kalinga, dear snake!' and sometimes you wanted me to become the Prince. Using both of us, you set your womb alight. Wooing my mind with smooth talk, you won your trial. Now, after using me, do you want to throw me away like a spent firebrand?

SAMPIGE. My body is not a commodity, Kalinga. For you that child may be an extension of your pride in yourself, but for me it is a wound you have given me.

KALINGA. It is difficult to understand you, woman.

SAMPIGE. Now I am worried for your life, and I am telling you, escape from here at once.

KALINGA. I have come here for the last time to tell you something, then I'll go. If I don't tell you, I may not even be able to die.

SAMPIGE. Why do you talk like this?

KALINGA. It is true, Sampige. Who else do I have but you?

SAMPIGE. Are you afraid, Kalinga?

KALINGA. Of whom, of the Prince? When I see him, I don't feel angry at all. I don't know why. Maybe my own entrails continue in him. Maybe we were brothers in a previous birth.

SAMPIGE. You wanted to tell me something. Tell me, I will listen.

BHAGAVATA. A frightful shadow, dear,
is haunting me;
an eagle is stalking me,
biding his time.

KALINGA. Listen, Sampige. I am surprised at how I have spent so many days with you. I started feeling that I was desiring some shadow beyond you, or that I had caused it some pain. Whenever I lay with you, that shadow beyond came to tease me. All these days I forgot it only in the momentary happiness of the body. I mean to embrace you in such a way that not even air can slip between us, but between us there remains a huge empty space. And in that space the dark shadow appears, beckoning to me. Before, I saw your body. Now I see nothing but the shadow. That shadow is the truth between us, I feel.

PRINCE (*from outside*). Close everything. Let a soldier with a weapon stand at each window and passageway. Remember, the enemy is a wizard who can take on any form he wants. Lady, open the door!

KALINGA. Now my mind is lighter. I will go now, lady. Open the door.

SAMPIGE. I will open the door slowly, singing a lullaby. Escape by the gutter. No one is standing that side.

BHAGAVATA. Cobra with his seven hoods,
in every hood a diamond gem,
snake entwined in a girl's plait,
in her plait adorned with jasmine,
sleeping cobra, hushabye,
hush, our Cobra King, hushabye![3]

3 An alternative and longer version of this song is included in the Appendix.

SCENE 14

The Prince and Awali.

BHAGAVATA. Open the door, you harlot!
Who are you playing around with?
I'll chop that rogue in pieces, roared the Prince.

AWALI. When the door was opened, there was nobody inside. Even when we searched according to your orders, in every nook and cranny, nobody was caught.

PRINCE. Did even a worm escape?

AWALI. Only a snake escaped by the gutter drain. We who were ready to hunt men thought that if we chased the snake, the enemy might escape, so we didn't go after it.

PRINCE. What was that snake like?

AWALI. When it got down into the garden, it threaded its way, like a stream flowing. Then, as if concerned that someone might see it, it looked around, moving its hood. And the hood was really very impressive

PRINCE. Were there not memories of joys devoured in its eye?

AWALI. We could not see its eye, friend.

PRINCE. When you saw it, did it not seem born in heaven?

AWALI. Yes. It moved with the poise of a thousand kings.

PRINCE. Did it shine in the sunlight, like a comet walking the earth?

AWALI. It shimmered like wheat, and its head was like lightning. Moving like the emperor of the forest, as if to show us the grandeur of the darkness, it disappeared inside a darkness filled anthill.

PRINCE. Was this not the same snake which the Queen took on her body that day at the trial?

AWALI. How can I tell, friend? I am not properly informed about animals.

PRINCE. Fool! Just as you could detect Jawali's secret pleasures, I too can detect the enthusiasm of that snake wherever it moves. Its royal poise proves that it is the same snake as the one which was there on the day of the trial. And if it is definitely the snake of the trial, then it is also definitely my enemy. He can take on any form he wills, and now, scared, he has run away as a snake. Go! If he enters an anthill, set fire to the anthill. If he enters the forest, set fire to that too. Even if you have to mix poison with the air we breathe, he must be caught and killed.

AWALI. I am going. (*Exits*.)

BHAGAVATA. Aha, she came, Siri Sampige,
lover inside and Queen outside,
deceit in female form came out, came out.

Sampige enters.

SAMPIGE. What is this, my lord? You appear to be prepared for battle.

PRINCE. Lady, do not cover up the truth with smooth talk. Tell me, did not a snake escape from here just now?

SAMPIGE. Yes.

PRINCE. Is it the same snake that moved around on your body on the day of the trial?

SAMPIGE. Yes.

PRINCE. Speak, then! Is not that snake your lover?

SAMPIGE. Yes.

PRINCE. In that case, what you have been doing all this time is immoral.

SAMPIGE. At last you have come to know of it. I am glad. I was wondering all the time how I could reveal it to you.

PRINCE. You cheated the Elders, you cheated everyone. You wounded them in their faith in you, didn't you? Your name which has been that of a goddess of town and temple will become a term of abuse for the whole country, do you know that?

SAMPIGE. That is your ill fortune. My immorality started, my lord, when you forgot the body and began craving for the god, and slipped away from our bed. I who was lying on the bed, counting the rafters in the roof and sighing, never noticed when you slipped away. I searched for you, but wherever I searched, in the palace garden, or in the words you spoke, you were not to be found. In the end, you saw the god by taking handfuls of water from the pond. I too took a handful of water, and there was a god in my handful too, but if he turned out not to be the same god as yours, is it my fault?

PRINCE. Do you know the punishment for immorality?

SAMPIGE. I am already half-widow, my lord. You can't understand the grief of one who is always half a widow! When you split yourself, you split me also. When you are before me, my body is widowed. When I am with him, lying with him, my mind is widowed. Thus I am always half-widow. There is nothing to equal such a torture. My sorrow is that no one understands me. I am alone. Afraid of loneliness, I search for a companion. But all the companions to be had are half-men. Was I born for half-men? I was born for and I am seeking the wholeness of the linga of the god Shiva. But what fell to my lot was a child born illicitly to an incomplete being. A child born to a widow. You have come here to kill the woman who gave birth to an illegitimate child? Look, I am ready!

Enter Awali.

AWALI. Friend, the trace of the enemy, has been found. He is hiding in an anthill. The soldiers are already digging up the anthill.

PRINCE. Lady, I have better work for my weapons. After beheading my enemy, I will come and dispose of you. Do not hope that I will die in battle. Since I have no brother, I cannot die.

The Prince and Awali exit.

SAMPIGE. Now I am a complete widow.

SCENE 15

A battlefield. The Prince and Kalinga face each other.

BHAGAVATA. You who lay with my woman,
You who polluted my lineage,
till I kill you I will not cease, roared the Prince.

PRINCE. Are you not the one who came like a wizard and lay as an adulterer with my woman? Are you not the dog who has polluted my lineage? Until I have killed such an adulterous thief as you, how can my weapons rest quietly? Come and give battle, lowest of the low!

BHAGAVATA. In the mirrors of eyes, I have seen you.
You are like my other self;
anger at you will not rise in me,
brother, perhaps in a previous birth.

KALINGA. Keep away, Prince! I am not one who is afraid to fight. I remember seeing you many times in a mirror. Pity wells up in me whenever I see you. Give me time, Prince, before battle, so I can think why I feel so troubled.

BHAGAVATA. Coiling up like a snake—
I don't understand this disguise—
I am your destiny's eagle,
resist, he said.

PRINCE. You who cheat by taking on any form that suits you, you need more time? You are scared for your life, shrinking, and coiling up, but none of your plots will succeed any longer. Look, the eagle of your destiny is going to fall on you now. If you have courage, defend yourself!

KALINGA. Prince, do not provoke my pride. You are delicate. You have only read about killing in poetry. Give me once, only once, a chance to look you in the eyes.

PRINCE. To do that would be the same as to give you a rope to tie my hands with. So what now? Are you going to fight or are you going to die like a coward? Look out, fight!

BHAGAVATA. Enraging each other, fighting, with roars their bravery flaunting both fought mightily their awful battle. At last, the Snake King's entrails aching, he opposed his foe less strongly. The Prince like thunder felled him, stamping on his body. Gazing at the sky's distance, life flew from the Snake spirit. In his open eyes, the Prince saw a wonder unforgettable. Looking there—ah ha—himself he felt his spine's knot slipping. 'My entrails have gone cold,' he said, coming to the palace.

SCENE 16

The palace. The Queen Mother is waiting for the Prince.

BHAGAVATA. News of victory can't make her happy, she remembers all her nightmares. With eyes wet, Mother was waiting at home.

QUEEN MOTHER. Even after hearing the news of the Prince's victory, my mind is anxious. If I shut my eyes I see only bad dreams, and if I open them bad omens arouse the fears in the depths. The palace is reverberating in silence, like a thunderstruck tree. Look, the Prince has come.

The Prince enters and offers his salutations to his Mother.

My child, may you be victorious over a thousand such enemies.

PRINCE. This is not such a great victory, Mother. (*He feels pain and sits down.*)

QUEEN MOTHER. No, my son. I never thought the Queen could cheat like this.

PRINCE. Where is Siri Sampige, Mother?

QUEEN MOTHER. She must be hiding in some corner, covering her shameless face. Do such people not commit suicide, son? I feel that at this moment the Queen should be with me. What kind of Queen is she now? She lost that position at the moment when she polluted the lineage. Should you look at her evil face at such a time of gladness like this, my child? There is something private I want to talk to her about. I, your mother, am with you. Is that not enough? You stay with me. Let her come too. Who is there?

SERVANT (*entering*). Lord, what is your command?

PRINCE. Ask the Queen to come. And call Awali too. I must have a word with him.

SERVANT. Awali died, my lord.

PRINCE. Awali died? When? How?

SERVANT. When you were fighting, Awali came running to us shouting, 'Alas, I am tripping over her hair, free me, free me'. We, who were busy watching your war did not pay any attention. Moreover, his feet were not tangled with hair. He kept running and went towards the lake which you visit every day. Meanwhile, as expected, you killed the enemy. I too ran towards the lake to tell him this joyful news. Awali had already begun to climb the tree on the bank that bends over the water. The tree's reflection was in the water. Awali's reflection had appeared too. Suddenly, he remembered Jawali and the quarrel and he thought that the one in the water was Jawali. Seeing Jawali, he grinned at him menacingly. In the water, Jawali too laughed to show that he was not afraid. He too laughed, and raised his arm, threatening to strike. The other did the same. He clenched his teeth and indicated that he would strangle the other. The other did the same. He became extremely angry and determined to kill, he jumped right into the lake. I watched all this, standing on the bank. I thought that he was probably miming your fight. But he drowned after having drunk so much water. He did not come up at all, my lord.

PRINCE (*agitated*). Go at once and ask the Queen to come, quick.

SERVANT. Very well, my lord. (*Exit*.)

PRINCE. How is my son, the Prince, Mother?

QUEEN MOTHER. You are tired after the fight. Take some rest. It is already dark outside. Your mind will be lighter when you get up in the morning. If you want, you can see Sampige tomorrow.

PRINCE. Mother, are you saying that tomorrow will dawn?

QUEEN MOTHER. What kind of a question is that my child? Tomorrow will dawn, but not as usual. Right and wrong will be in their proper places. The darkness of doubt will have passed away. Do you know, there will not be a corner of the palace where the light does not fall. Dawn has only to awaken, and the buds of a new world will open out. All the old grief will blossom into smiles. I myself will show you, king upon your throne, the new world.

PRINCE. Mother.

QUEEN MOTHER. Son.

PRINCE. Do you have faith in me, Mother?

QUEEN MOTHER. From now onwards I will believe every word you say, my child. Because I did not believe your words on the day of trial, all these terrible things came about. A mother who does not believe her son's words is virtually a black goddess. But I will never forgive Siri Sampige for cheating like this.

PRINCE. Now there are no secrets between us, may I ask you a question, Mother?

QUEEN MOTHER. Ask, my child.

PRINCE. Listen calmly. My navel is growing cold. My spine is loosening.

QUEEN MOTHER (*horrified*). What? What did you say, son? Who is there? Servants! Someone come quickly!

PRINCE. Don't shout, Mother. Please listen to me.

QUEEN MOTHER. Watching your face I am becoming scared, my son. I am a sinner not to have realized at once. I thought it was the fatigue of the fight. Did he wound you?

PRINCE. Listen, Mother. Even my death depends on the truth that you must tell me. You must reveal the hidden truth now.

QUEEN MOTHER. What is it? Ask me, my child.

PRINCE. Is it true that I have no brother to be heir to what I am heir to, Mother?

QUEEN MOTHER. Do you doubt your Mother's word? Look, I swear on the family god . . .

PRINCE. Oaths and vows are not required, Mother. You can simply tell me.

QUEEN MOTHER. You have no brother, my son.

PRINCE. I am to die together with my brother, is that not so?

QUEEN MOTHER. Yes.

PRINCE. Suppose I have no brother?

QUEEN MOTHER. Then you will not die.

BHAGAVATA. Splitting ourselves we became two body and mind became separate.

PRINCE. No other may have been born from your womb, but when the one son who was born from you split himself in two, did not the other part which came to life become my brother and the sharer of my inheritance? Tell me, Mother, the other who came to life when I split myself, who was he? When I asked all of you, you said it was a devil, an evil spirit. Was it not the Snake King Kalinga, Mother?

QUEEN MOTHER (*stricken*). Yes. What came out of the pot before you was a snake!

PRINCE. Mother, think carefully. Was he not the same snake who was used for the trial?

QUEEN MOTHER. Perhaps . . .

PRINCE. Certainly he was the same, Mother. He did not fight with me as he should have. He said, 'Somehow I cannot get angry with you. Give me a chance to look into your eyes.' But I refused his request and fought with him, and since his heart was not in the fight, I easily killed him. He died opening his eyes and looking at the sky. I could not control my curiosity and looked into his eyes.

QUEEN MOTHER. What did you see, son?

PRINCE. In his eyes was reflected the lovely blue sky. I saw in the sky an eagle and a snake flying together. The snake, which had within it all the dark black secrets of the nether world, was not in the claws of the eagle but was wound around its neck and body in friendship. The duality of the snake and the eagle had been erased and they had become one. The mercy of Shiva's divine eyes was falling on them in the form of the sun's golden rays. What I saw now was like a snake playing in the sky, opening his hood. Only the snake was visible, having completely taken over the eagle, and it looked as if the snake with its open hood had sprouted wings and was flying. Then that eagle, with its forehead set to the streaming sun, climbed fearlessly into the eternity of the sky.

QUEEN MOTHER. Son, what do you mean by this?

PRINCE. The Queen would have understood all these things. Siri Sampige has not committed any wrong, Mother. When I split myself, we got separated into body and mind. Kalinga became my body, I became his mind. Siri Sampige became pregnant by my body.

QUEEN MOTHER (*in wonder and repentance*). True, son. That is why whenever he wanted he was able to take on your shape. Son, the Queen has done no wrong. Alas! Sinner that I am, I forgot what I was doing. Now I am afraid for your life. Who is there?

PRINCE. I have already killed myself, Mother. Look, the Queen has come. Come Siri Sampige.

Sampige approaches.

QUEEN MOTHER. Is no one coming? Siri Sampige, you stay at the Prince's side. I will go and bring the doctor. (*Exit.*)

PRINCE. You who were being burned in the fire of misunderstanding . . . at last I feel I have understood.

SAMPIGE. Are you well, my lord?

PRINCE. Queen, how is the Prince?

SAMPIGE. He is sleeping quietly. How are you, my lord?

PRINCE. Did you hear the news?

SAMPIGE. Yes, my lord. You killed Kalinga.

PRINCE. Have our prince perform the last rites for him. For me also.

SAMPIGE. My lord!

PRINCE. Listen. See to it that our son does not split himself. (*He dies.*)

Curtain.

APPENDIX

Hushabye, our Cobra lord!

Kalinga is the name of a cobra
who has seven hoods,
seven gems like seven sun cubs
sit in his seven hoods.

He waves his hoods and tail
whenever he sees a girl;
to see a little girl with oiled plaits
makes Kalinga very pleased.

He entwines his body in the plaits
and swings like a plait himself;
if the girl has jasmine in her hair
he nods off happily.
Hushabye, our Cobra lord!

If he sees a shadow, he flies into a rage
and hits it with his hood,
flings his gems at the fleeing shadow,
flicking his forked tongue.

Once our Kalinga in fresh sunshine
stretched out his length;
an eagle's shadow as big as a mountain
touched his snake body.

He burned with anger, his eyes threw sparks,
he displayed his seven hoods,
and thrashed that shadow wherever it went
with his hoods, like a thunderbolt.

Thrashing, from his hoods the fresh blood flowed;
his hoods shriveled and shrank,
his eyes became charcoal, his body a rag
his tongue a loose thread—
hushabye, our Cobra lord!
Bury him in flowers, bury him in dreams—
hushabye, our Cobra lord!
Shoo shoo, eagle, fly far away,
my child is sleeping sound.
Hushabye, our Cobra lord!

FOLK THEATRE AS I SEE IT

I am often asked for my reading of what folk theatre is, its relevance to me, to my times and to my people.

Let me begin with myself. I belong geographically to a village, and sociologically to what was considered to be an oppressed, uneducated class. I am, therefore, a folk person simply because I cannot be anything else. (I stress this point because in these last ten years a kind of 'folksiness' has become the 'in' thing among the sophisticated urban class.) The first long poem I wrote, *Helatena Kela,* was entirely drawn from my soil. Looking at it twenty-five years later, I find that most of my writing is thematically connected with that long poem. This is not a statement of a painful effort at thematic consistency; nor is it, I hope, a statement of creative bankruptcy. The sheer comprehensiveness and opulence of the experience as it formed itself in *Helatena Kela* has given me structures and approaches adequate to my most varied needs as an artist and as a man trying to articulate the creative urge of my people. I might make bold to state that the kind of folk medium which made *Helatena Kela* possible also made *Jokumaraswami* and other plays of mine possible. I have a feeling, which has endured these many years and will endure hereafter, that I am handling an art which is *total*.

I realize that my claim is bound to be controversial, especially as a statement towards the end of the twentieth century; and so I wish to discuss and elaborate on it. To begin in a simple fashion, the calendar to me is not an important calibration of change in matters of sensibility. People sense relevance of experience according to needs, both imaginative and emotional, which are much more indirect and subtle. The durability or the transitoriness of experience and the art it engenders is something that occurs out of the sociocultural needs of a people, their anguishes, their puzzlements and their exhilarations. The artist who draws his creativity strongly from his people articulates and places that sense of relevance. It is a fact that my people, even today, live largely governed by feudal values and have structures and textures of living which belong to other, previous times. I am not being apologetic or critical. An artist uses fact as stuff, in doing so, he might affect a very slight change in his people, in himself and in their relations. Sometimes, if he is fortunate, he might alight on structures, tones, myths and symbols which are so fundamental and hence so powerful that issues like contemporaneity simply do not feature where he functions. For instance, I began by telling a story of fertility, impotence and drought in *Helatena Kela* and have continued to work around those themes in all my plays. T. S. Eliot and Yeats, both products of a Western and largely urban culture, and prime spokesmen of literary modernism, nevertheless had similar themes at the centre of their *oeuvres*. Believe it or not, I draw my stuff from my village, not from Eliot or Yeats. What I mean to say is that there are aspects of the human condition so fundamental that they ever oppress, ever stimulate, and in this, they lie under and beyond time and place.

There is another sense in which I want to look at the term 'total'. One might say that human society has passed through various stages or one might say that human society is found in various conditions. There is that society in which, for many reasons, the quality of living is one of sanctioned inhibition; of suppressed drives, emotional or sexual. The only area of living in which inhibitions are necessarily removed is the area related to religion. We find in such societies that a normally inhibited member breaks out of the restraining structures only in a situation which has religious sanction. Hence the phenomena of all kinds of frenzied behaviour associated with religious rituals in societies otherwise inhibited. And the frenzy includes superhuman feats and self-mortification, as well as sex. In short, these are necessary outlets for the survival and sanity of that society. Proceeding further, we also observe that the distinction here between the realm of entertainment and the realm of actual living is as clear as that between normal living and participation in religious ritual. Paradoxically, it is because of this very definite separation that the realm of entertainment in such a society assumes a total and microcosmic character—microcosmic in the sense that entertainment then reflects all the creative urges and needs in the world outside. Thus it is at once a phenomenon both of concentration and comprehensiveness. And therefore, the folk theatre includes dance, drama, narration, song, sex, death and religion. Most importantly, it is not only the actors who are separate from the world outside but the audience of the play as well. For the audience of the folk play *participates* in the play. Indeed, both the actors and the audience are co-participants in what is ultimately a shared religious ritual in the form of a play. The shoddiest production of a bayalata begins with prayer and ends with the audience as well as the players going to a temple early in the morning. Against this background, cliched remarks against song and dance in our plays are irrelevant. These remarks arise out of a different understanding of the function of entertainment, in societies different from the kind of societies I have described. In what might be called a modern society, there is conscious and unconscious secularization: more and more of the important happenings in a man's life are detached from an overall religious framework. Simultaneously, we see that the area of religious influence narrows and religion becomes almost a profession, functioning at certain socially sanctioned centres. Art, dance, drama, song, spread out into society at large, and in doing so, they also get separated. A Londoner finds his dance, song, drama and religion at different places. A man from my village looks for all these things together. To simplify: Ibsen is impossible in my village; but, may I add, he should not be possible.

I shall try to explain this phenomenon in somewhat different terms. A criticism is often made, and not entirely without justification, that our plays, being full of action-retarding and theme-diluting music and dance and poetry, are escapist. While there might be some substance in this criticism when it relates to some of our secular plays and films, it cannot apply to our folk theatre. The entertainment in the folk theatre, it should be obvious by now, is importantly compensatory in nature. It is there that a man who lives a deprived existence in many ways under sociocultural inhibitions, sees himself as full, and rising above the limitations of his deprived existence. And the religious framework in which this important release and completion takes place indicates a sanction which encompasses his micro as well as macro realms. On the other hand, the urbanite (my Londoner) has a choice between entertainment and religion, and in entertainment itself a choice of various kinds and levels. If he attends a musical or a strip show, his act is escapist. If there is music or the stripping of Draupadi in a bayalata, the import is different. It is fundamentally religious and compensatory. That the symptoms of escapism and the signals of a folk play appear similar is merely an accident of structural similarity. One has to think alertly to see the difference in import.

I am asked sometimes what I think about the future of folk theatre. Will it be valid in the coming world of computers and *Star Wars*? I am obliged to repeat what I have suggested before. Folk theatre, like language, is always adequate to the needs of its users at any given point in time. It will be valid as long as its users need it to be. If change occurs with the slow gradualness of history, it will survive into future times. If apocalyptic change occurs, it will not survive. But then, neither will its users.

Chandrasekhar Kambar
1991

GANESHA [illegible] you know how he came into being? There was a time [illegible] made friends with me. [illegible] he could [illegible] Once I found a strand of hair belonging to [illegible] said it was the form of a donkey. [illegible]

SAMBA [illegible]

GANESHA [illegible] donkey [illegible]

SAMBA [illegible] giving you the donkey [illegible]

[illegible]

GANESHA [illegible]

SHIVA What was your blessing?

GANESHA What do you want?

SHIVA Only that I should get the girl I desire.

GANESHA The donkey will help you get the girl [illegible]

SAMBA [illegible]

GANESHA [illegible]